Sources of Strength

Also by Jimmy Carter

Living Faith

Turning Point: A Candidate, a State, and a Nation Come of Age

Talking Peace: A Vision for the Next Generation

An Outdoor Journal

Everything to Gain: Making the Most of the Rest of Your Life
(with Rosalynn Carter)

The Blood of Abraham: Insights into the Middle East

Keeping Faith: Memoirs of a President

A Government as Good as Its People

Why Not the Best?

Poetry
Always a Reckoning

For Children
The Little Baby Snoogle-Fleejer
(with Amy Carter)

Sources of Strength

Meditations on Scripture for a Living Faith

Jimmy Carter

TIMES BOOKS
RANDOM HOUSE

To Amy Carter and Jim Wentzel

 Published in the United States by Times Books, a division of Random House, Inc., New York, and simultaneously in Canada by Random House of Canada Limited, Toronto.
ISBN 0-8129-2944-6

Book design by Maura Fadden Rosenthal/Mspace
Printed in the United States of America

Preface

Sources of Strength is a companion to *Living Faith.** In fact, when I began writing the earlier book, I intended it to be like this one, a collection of some of the favorite Bible lessons I have taught. As the text evolved during the spring of 1996, however, it became increasingly obvious that the overall impact of my personal faith on my life and thinking needed first to be explained. The resulting book—part spiritual autobiography, part Christian teaching—was *Living Faith.*

Now, a year later, I have returned to my original plan. Although I began teaching Sunday School classes when I was eighteen years old, I've retained written outlines and transcripts of entire texts only during the past twenty years. I asked Karl Weber, a fine editor, to help me choose some of the more interesting ones. Together, we abbreviated each of the forty-five-minute talks down to a few pages, and I added some more recent personal anecdotes to help illustrate key points.

Nine of the Bible lessons I've included here came from

* New York: Times Books, 1996.

when I taught adult Sunday School at First Baptist Church in Washington, the church our family attended while I was president. Like other Christians, our family needed spiritual fellowship, not special recognition or honors, so as much as possible we were treated the same as any other members of the church. There was never any advance announcement when I was to teach, and I didn't even know that the lessons had been recorded until after I left the White House.

Nowadays, I teach about two-thirds of the Sundays at Maranatha Baptist Church in our hometown of Plains, Georgia. We have only about thirty families as active members, and most of them are teaching other classes, keeping the nursery, and managing church affairs while I teach. However, there are usually several hundred visitors who come to hear my lessons. I'm sure that they have many motivations, including the desire to meet a former president, to hear what a politician has to say about the Scriptures, to explore or debate ideas expressed in my previous books, to seek a new religious experience, or just to enjoy an unusual Sunday morning outing. Some have never before attended a religious service, and others are pastors, scholars, or well-known authors of religious books. About a fifth are Southern Baptists, but most are members of other Christian traditions, Protestant, Catholic, and Orthodox. We also welcome Jews, Muslims, and adherents of different faiths—and some who have no faith but perhaps are searching for one.

For me, and for many of those in the classes, there is a surprising element of interest and even excitement in exploring Scripture together. I have chosen the texts in this book from those that stimulated the more intriguing discussions in class. I have arranged the meditations to provide some aspects of both continuity and diversity of ideas, but each really stands on its own. Since I have almost a completely new group each Sunday, I do repeat some favorite themes. There are, therefore, a few repetitions of both ideas and texts in this book, but the basic thrust of each lesson is meant to be distinct. Some of them should be comprehensible on first reading, while others will require some contemplation.

There are fifty-two meditations in this book, one for each week of the year. But don't feel constrained to pace yourself accordingly. Since the Scripture selections and comments are so brief, my hope is that you will supplement what I have presented with further study of the Bible and associated commentaries. The book includes passages from both the Hebrew and Greek texts of Scripture. I refer to the two portions of the Bible as the Old Testament and New Testament, the traditional designations I have always used in my classes.

I have thoroughly enjoyed recapitulating the lessons I've taught over the years; for me, the ancient texts always come alive when I explore them with a searching heart. I hope they will be for you, as they have been for me, sources of strength.

Jimmy Carter
Plains, Georgia
June 1997

Contents

INTRODUCTION

Why Should We Read the Bible?

> All scripture is inspired by God, and profitable for teaching, for reproof, for correction, for training in righteousness; that the man of God may be adequate, equipped for every good work.
>
> 2 TIMOTHY 3:16–17

In December 1996, I was on *The Tonight Show* discussing my book *Living Faith.* The host, Jay Leno, showed a videotape of some extemporaneous interviews with people he met on the streets of Los Angeles in which he asked them questions about the Bible. The answers were both hilarious and disturbing. For example, there were some who thought that the first commandment was "freedom of speech," that Eve was created from an apple, and that Noah's ark landed on Mount Everest. I played the tape for my Sunday School class, and subsequently someone sent me a news article containing funny comments by students about the Bible, including these:

> "Noah's wife was called Joan of Ark."
>
> "Lot's wife was a pillar of salt by day and a ball of fire by night."
>
> "Seventh commandment: Thou shalt not admit adultery."
>
> "Epistles were wives of the apostles."
>
> "A Christian has only one wife. This is called monotony."

One middle-aged woman interviewed by Leno responded proudly that she had a Bible in her house. When he asked her to name the last time she had opened it, she said she thought it was when she had used it in a college course. If we're honest, many of us might have to say the same. But if we'd bought a new automobile for which we had saved for several years, there is little doubt that we would study the manual until we mastered it and would refer back to the text whenever we had a problem. I have several thick books on how to use my computer and printer, a CD-ROM encyclopedia, and other books on how to explore the Internet. The authors of *Word for Dummies*, *Windows 95 for Dummies*, and other similar texts have gotten rich. Yet the operating manual for life on earth is sadly neglected. We don't really need a *Bible for Dummies*, since the meaning of the inspired word of God is clear enough to meet our needs. The Scriptures are full of interesting, shocking, helpful, and inspiring stories—but, unfortunately, they go unexplored by many of us.

The theologian Paul Tillich says that religion is the search for the truth about ourselves, and how we relate to God and to other people. Since this is the essence of life, it is obviously valuable for us to understand these relationships. One way is through the study of the Holy Word of God—the Bible.

Another theologian, Karl Barth, said that our relationship to the Bible is like being inside a house and gazing out at a group of people on the street. They are all looking toward the sky with faces expressing delight, wonder, pain, hope, guilt, or joy. They are obviously intrigued by something remarkable, perhaps miraculous or mysterious, but out of our view. For thousands of years, these have been the reactions of hundreds of millions of people who read Genesis, Isaiah, Micah, Luke, the letters of Paul, or Revelation. Shouldn't we be curious about what those millions have seen?

Paul's letter to the young Timothy, quoted at the beginning of this introduction, was probably written before any of the four Gospels. These two verses are the most succinct biblical description of the value of the Scriptures. "The inspired word of God" doesn't mean that every translation or interpretation of Scripture is literally accurate. We can select an isolated verse here and another there and use them to justify almost any of our personal prejudices. In fact, the earliest and most constant conflict between Jesus Christ and certain religious leaders of his time occurred because they were inclined to focus on the individual verses, or their interpretation of them, instead of on the essence of God's message. They were so concerned about exactly what one could do on the

Sabbath, what was acceptable to eat or to wear, and the detailed procedures for worshiping and making religious donations that they forgot that God was a creator filled with love, grace, and forgiveness.

Let's look at some other words in Paul's advice about reading Scripture. "Reproof" means constructive criticism or self-analysis, and "correction" means improvement of our behavior or our priorities in life. "Training in righteousness" means learning to do God's will, or becoming more like Christ. The meaning of the other words is clear, but "equipped for every good work" warrants a few more thoughts.

All of us can try to live an average life—nothing special, but good enough to get along and to make us feel self-satisfied. But an important reason to study the Scriptures is to help each of us define and strive for a transcendent life—a life that reaches above and beyond what is normally expected of us. From Scripture, we can learn how Jesus Christ lived and what he set forth as proper priorities for human existence. We are aware of this opportunity in moments of exaltation or inspiration, when we are embarrassed by our own inadequacies, or perhaps when we are in total despair. The Bible offers concrete guidance for overcoming our weaknesses and striving toward the transcendent life for which we were created.

It's almost always helpful to share our studies or questions with someone else in whom we have confidence. For the last twenty years, Rosalynn and I have read a portion of the Bible each night. When we're together, we alternate reading aloud, and when we're apart we enjoy knowing that we are contemplating the same text. We have been through the entire Bible several times in Spanish, to practice our foreign language as we nurture ourselves spiritually.

After a personal witnessing experience with Eloy Cruz, an admirable Cuban pastor who had surprising rapport with very poor immigrants from Puerto Rico, I asked him for the secret of his success. He was modest and embarrassed, but he finally said, "Señor Jimmy, we only need to have two loves in our lives: for God, and for the person who happens to be in front of us at any time." That simple yet profound theology has been a great help to me in understanding the Scriptures. In essence, the whole Bible is an explanation of those two loves.

The Word Became Flesh

CHAPTER ONE

What It Takes to Be a Christian

> The jailer asked, "What must I do to be saved?"
>
> Paul answered, "Believe in the Lord Jesus, and you will be saved—you and your household."
>
> ACTS 16:30–31

Many people have asked the question the jailer does here, and Paul's simple response is the answer that has been accepted by almost two billion Christians living around the world today.

As a young man, I joined other members of our church in carrying this same message about Jesus Christ to the families in our rural community who were not Christians. This was very difficult for me, because I was always doubtful about the reception we would receive. I usually knew the families well, so I was somewhat embarrassed about implying that I was superior in some way, having knowledge or a privileged position that they didn't.

However, the company of another man always strengthened me. We were well versed in the rudimentary tenets of what we called "The Plan of Salvation," which was the basis for our brief presentation.

Later, beginning in the mid-1960s, I traveled to more distant places for a week or so as a volunteer lay missionary, joining others in Pennsylvania, Massachusetts, and in the suburbs of Atlanta to visit homes and share our faith in Christ. We approached each family with sincere prayers, and learned to rely on the presence of the Holy Spirit to overcome our timidity and uncertainties. In other words, we just did our best and had faith enough to relax and leave the results to God.

The Plan of Salvation is still an integral part of my weekly Bible lessons. I often outline it briefly when I receive a question about the nature of Christian faith from a visitor or when the lesson text has an evangelical meaning—as most of them do. In this first meditation, I want to share the Plan of Salvation with you, relying more on a few passages of Scripture than on my own words.

1. *God loves all of us.* "For God so loved the world that he gave his only Son, so that everyone who believes in him may not perish, but may have everlasting life" (John 3:16). "For God, who is rich in mercy, out of the great love with which he loved us even when we were dead through our trespasses, made us alive together

with Christ—by grace you have been saved" (Ephesians 2:4–5).

2. *All of us are sinners.* Some of us may be satisfied with the way we are, feeling that we don't need God's mercy, but the Holy Scriptures are clear: "All we like sheep have gone astray; we have turned every one to his own way" (Isaiah 53:6). "There is no one who is righteous, not even one" (Romans 3:10). And "All have sinned, and fall short of the glory of God" (Romans 3:23).

3. *Sin separates us from God.* What are the consequences of our violating God's moral code? There is a clear and disturbing answer: "For the wages of sin is death" (Romans 6:23).

4. *We cannot save ourselves.* Only God can save us, through our faith. Even the Hebrew patriarch Abraham did not earn his righteousness before God; it came because of his belief, or faith: "For if Abraham was justified by works, he has something to boast about, but not before God. For the scripture says, 'Abraham believed God, and it was reckoned to him as righteousness' " (Romans 4:2–3 and Genesis 15:6).

"For by grace are you saved through faith, and this is not your own doing; it is the gift of God—not the result of works, so that no one may boast" (Ephesians 2:8–9).

5. *Jesus came to remove the barrier of sin.* "But God proves his love for us in that while we still were sinners Christ died for us" (Romans 5:8). "He himself bore our sins in his body on the cross, so that, free from sins, we

might live for righteousness; by his wounds you have been healed" (1 Peter 2:24).

6. *It is through our faith in Christ that we receive these blessings.* "If you confess with your lips that Jesus is Lord and believe in your heart that God raised him from the dead, you will be saved. For one believes with the heart and so is justified, and one confesses with the mouth and so is saved" (Romans 10:9–10).

These are the premises that all Christians have accepted. Some people may think this path to salvation is too simple and easy—that something else must be required for us to receive God's mercy and everlasting life. After all, most of the achievements in life—education, a good family, a successful career—require hard work, persistence, and sacrifice. Yet God's forgiveness and blessings are given to us freely, by pure grace.

This mistaken attitude reminds me of the reaction of the Syrian general Naaman, who went to the prophet Elisha to be cured of leprosy. Without leaving his tent, Elisha sent word that Naaman needed only to bathe in the little Jordan River seven times to be cured. The powerful man stormed away, furious at the simplicity of the prescription. But his servants said, "If the prophet had commanded you to do something difficult, would you not have done it? How much more, when all he said to you was, 'Wash, and be clean'? So he went down and immersed himself seven times in the Jordan, according to the word of the man of God; his flesh was restored like the flesh of a young boy, and he was clean" (2 Kings 5:13–14).

The simple but profound fact is that our lives can be changed—beginning now—by professing our faith in Jesus Christ. The rest of this book will explore the fascinating, exciting, and remarkable ramifications of this basic, life-giving truth.

Chapter Two

A Humble Servant

All we like sheep have gone astray; we have turned every one to his own way; and the Lord hath laid on him the iniquity of us all. He was oppressed, and he was afflicted, yet he opened not his mouth: he is brought as a lamb to the slaughter, and as a sheep before her shearers is dumb, so he openeth not his mouth.

Isaiah 53:6–7

Christians are, by definition, "little Christs." As such, we ought to know as much about Jesus as possible and to emulate him as fully as we can. As we know, even the disciples who were with him every day did not really understand what aspects of his life they were supposed to adopt. It is interesting now to go back into the Old Testament, to correlate the prophecies with what we know from the Gospels about Jesus as a human being, and then try to apply this awareness to our own lives.

Although we Christians believe that a number of ancient prophets depicted the coming Messiah, the most fascinating descriptions come from the Book of Isaiah. Biblical scholars disagree about the authorship and meaning of the verses, but I believe that these were the words of the great prophet and that he was referring to Jesus as Messiah. One reason for this assessment is that Jesus, in his hometown synagogue, quoted directly from Isaiah and applied the prophecy to himself.

When invited to read from the Scripture, Jesus picked up the scroll and turned to this passage: " 'The spirit of the Lord is upon me because he has anointed me to bring good news to the poor; he has sent me to heal the brokenhearted, to preach deliverance to the captives, recovery of sight to the blind, to let the oppressed go free, to proclaim the year of the Lord.' Then he rolled up the scroll and said, 'Today this scripture has been fulfilled in your hearing' " (Luke 4:18–21).

The quoted words come from Isaiah 61:1–2. They lead us to examine other prophetic texts about Christ—how he lived, looked, and acted. We are inclined to think of our Lord as being tall, slender, and handsome. He was, we assume, an eloquent and convincing speaker, who attracted and retained loyal disciples and adoring crowds. In fact, almost all these images are incorrect, as an unbiased reading of the Gospels reveals.

There is a remarkably descriptive passage from Isaiah: "For he grew up before him like a tender shoot, like a root out of parched ground; he had no stately form or majesty that we should look at him, nor appearance that we should be attracted to him. He was despised and forsaken of men, a man of sorrows, and acquainted with grief; and like one from whom men hide their face, he was despised, and we did not esteem him. Surely our griefs he himself bore, and our sorrows he carried; . . . He was pierced through for our transgressions, he was crushed for our iniquities, . . . and by his scourging we are healed" (53:2–5).

Remember that Jesus came from a lowly family that could afford only two doves for an offering in the temple. Although he was charismatic, we can only imagine his physical appearance, which is never described in the New Testament. And what about the effectiveness of his preaching? At the end of his perfect life and three years of preaching, primarily to his apostles, they were not fully convinced. Confused and disillusioned by his trial and execution, which he had frequently predicted in clear language, they abandoned him when he needed them most.

It was only later, with Jesus' resurrection and the coming of the Holy Spirit, that his followers were personally transformed and remembered the events of his life as transcendent and inspirational. Now, in retrospect, we have the same perspective. We are able to correlate omnipotence, majesty, and judgment with humility, mercy, forgiveness, and love.

As Christians, we are servants of God. But does this mean that we are superior to others, self-sufficient, or naturally blessed with material riches? This question was answered repeatedly in the history of the Israelites. Although they were God's chosen people, they always failed when they became arrogant, decided they didn't need God, or defined success by selfish human standards. We Christians face the same temptations—and, like those ancient Jews, we frequently succumb.

Jesus came to explain these truths in human terms, so that we might comprehend them and apply them in our own lives. The most succinct description of Christ is as a suffering servant, and he tried to give his followers the proper definition of greatness: "But he that is greatest among you shall be your servant" (Matthew 23:11).

Looked at objectively, it is extraordinary that the symbol of Christianity is the cross—something like an electric chair, a hangman's noose, or a lethal hypodermic needle. How could the instrument of the most savage human executions be so greatly exalted? It is a vivid reminder of the humanity of Jesus, who sacrificed his own perfect life that we might know the blessing of God's mercy, forgiveness, and love.

CHAPTER THREE

Full of Grace and Truth

The Word became flesh and lived among us. We have seen his glory, the glory of the one and only Son, who came from the Father, full of grace and truth.

... No one has ever seen God, but God the only Son, who is at the Father's side, has made him known.

JOHN 1:14, 18

This is one of the most beautiful passages in the Bible. The description it offers of Christ is profound: mysterious yet comprehensible, simple yet filled with meaning. The longer we meditate on these words, the more they mean to us.

The verses quoted begin by saying that the Word—

meaning both Greek *logos*, standing for truth or wisdom, and the word of God, as given to the Jews through Moses—became "flesh." What more common yet descriptive word could we choose? Flesh—the very living stuff of which our bodies are made, the substance that makes up a pounding heart, or a working brain, or a grasping hand. The inexhaustible paradox of God as human is captured in that phrase. The Word became a fleshly person, like one of us, walking the dusty roads of Palestine; sleeping in the open with a stone or a rolled-up cloak for a pillow; eating, drinking, laughing with friends: the Word became flesh.

Yet this was no ordinary human but an extraordinary being, full of grace and truth. Here we have another word, *grace*, that conveys so much meaning in such a small space. Grace is unmerited favor, the undeserved gift of God's love and forgiveness, bestowed on us freely, unlimited and inexhaustible. Jesus Christ, in his teaching, his miracles, his life, death, and resurrection, embodies God's generosity to us: full of grace, indeed.

Isn't it remarkable to see God coming to earth in this form? Not as a triumphant ruler, riding a white horse and wearing a crown, leading an army to expel the hated Romans and fulfilling human desires or ambitions, but rather as one who epitomizes unlimited forgiveness, compassion, service, peace, and love. A man, yet God, who was there when the universe was created, knowing everything, totally powerful.

No one has ever seen God, John goes on to say, and of course this is true. People in all times and places have struggled to visualize God, and artists have depicted God in accordance with the customs of their societies. Michelangelo, for example, created my first physical image of God: white hair, a long, flowing beard, a white robe. This is the God I pictured when I was a child, sitting on a throne in heaven and keeping tabs on me, writing down in a book the good things and the bad things I did.

Yet we know that God is neither male nor female; only sexist assumptions make God into an old white-haired man. And our assumptions about God as judge need to be qualified and corrected as well. As John assures us: "But if we love each other, God lives in us and his love is made complete in us" (1 John 4:12). He makes the point this way: "Whoever does not love does not know God, because God is love" (4:8).

God is love: this is the first Bible verse many children learn by memory and the most succinct description in Scripture. Christ will indeed be our judge at the end of days, as he tells in the beautiful passage about separating the sheep and the goats (Matthew 25:31–46). But God's basic nature is not judgmental. God is love: *agape* love, forgiving love, love for those who are unattractive, those who don't deserve to be loved, those who don't love us back. God is love in its purest, most exalted, and most exciting, challenging, and difficult meaning. This is what Jesus came to earth to teach us, and this is why John describes him as full of grace.

But remember, too, the word John places in juxtaposition to grace: *truth.* Grace is gentle, grace is nice, but truth can be difficult to face. What is the truth about my life, or yours—judged not by human standards but by the standards of Jesus Christ? Have I lived in a way that is truly compatible with the teachings of the humble, human, yet all-loving and all-knowing God I have pledged to follow? This truth can be troubling, even humiliating—though *humbling* may be a better word.

But, fortunately, in John's Gospel, and in the life of Christ, grace and truth go together. If it weren't for the assurance of grace, how could we acknowledge the full truth about ourselves? We can depend upon the love and forgiveness of Jesus to correct and cleanse us. This, too, is part of John's beautiful and reassuring message.

Chapter Four

The Laughing Jesus

The chief priests and the elders came to him as he was teaching, and said, "By what authority do you these things?" . . . And Jesus answered, "I also will ask you one thing, which if you tell me, I will tell you by what authority I do these things. The baptism of John, whence was it? From heaven or of men?" And they reasoned together, saying, "If we shall say, 'From heaven,' he will say unto us, 'Why did you not then believe him?' But if we shall say, 'Of men,' we fear the people, for all hold John as a prophet." And they answered Jesus, and said, "We cannot tell." And he said unto them, "Neither will I tell you by what authority I do these things."

Matthew 21:23–27

I received several angry letters from readers of my book *Living Faith* because I commented there that Jesus could easily have substituted for Jay Leno or David Letterman on the late-night talk shows. My correspondents seemed to believe it was sacrilegious to think that Jesus Christ had a sense of humor. One person, however, sent me a copy of "The Laughing Jesus," a delightful painting that could very well have represented him and the bystanders after a witty exchange like the one just quoted.

It's a shame that so many people believe that Jesus was always solemn, and that therefore the proper demeanor for his followers is to be grim, stern, even haughty toward others. In fact, Jesus had a good time, and he encouraged his disciples to join him in enjoying life. There are numerous accounts of his going to parties and associating with a broad range of apparently carousing acquaintances. Jesus and his friends were chastised by the scribes and Pharisees: "Why do you eat and drink with publicans and sinners?" and later, "Why do the disciples of John fast often, and make prayers, and likewise the disciples of the Pharisees; but yours eat and drink?"

Jesus replied, in effect, that it was important for him to be a friend to sinners, who needed him, and that he and his disciples wanted to enjoy each other's company while they had a chance, because he would not always be with them.

I never knew anyone who had more close friends than my brother, Billy—probably ten for every one that I have. He had a great sense of humor, which sometimes got him into trouble. During the summer of 1976, after I had been nominated as the Democratic candidate for president, our hometown of Plains was filled with reporters, many of whom spent a lot of time around Billy's service station. They enjoyed and wrote down the idle and sometimes ribald statements they heard and, unfortunately, later used them as serious quotations to make Billy look foolish.

Earlier that year, before our family members were well known, a new reporter in town asked Billy if he didn't agree that he was somewhat peculiar. He replied, "My mother went into the Peace Corps when she was sixty-eight years old; my youngest sister is a holy-roly preacher; my other sister is eight years older than I am and spends half her time on a Harley-Davidson motorcycle; and my brother thinks he's going to be President of the United States! I'm the only one in the family who is normal!"

My mother was a lot like Billy. The following year, in January, I had just been inaugurated, walked down Pennsylvania Avenue, reviewed the parade with my family, and then begun to walk with my family, for the first time, toward the White House. Eager news reporters with cameras surrounded us, and my press secretary said, "Don't anyone stop to answer questions." Typically, Mama ignored him and stopped to talk to the press. The first question was "Miss Lillian, aren't you proud of your son?" Mama replied, "Which one?"

Billy and Mama enjoyed life and even on their deathbeds retained their equanimity and their sense of humor. As did Jesus', Billy's and Mama's joy and humor helped draw people together, assuaged sorrow, and, when necessary, deflated pride in a positive way.

It is good for us personally and as Christian witnesses to remember that, in spite of trials and tribulations, we should also enjoy life—more like Jesus and not like the scribes and Pharisees, solemn, proud, and inclined to judge others. Did Jesus laugh? Yes, he did—often, and with a full heart.

CHAPTER FIVE

The Special Message of Jesus

> You have heard that it has been said, "You shall love your neighbor, and hate your enemy!" But I say to you, "Love your enemies, bless them that curse you, do good to them that hate you, and pray for them which despitefully use you and persecute you."
>
> MATTHEW 5:43–44

On my bookshelf I have an interesting book that was published in 1978 called *The 100*, by Michael Hart. It is a ranking of the most influential persons in history. I disagree with a lot of Hart's opinions. For instance, he ranks Jesus third, behind Muhammad and Isaac Newton (Buddha,

Confucius, and St. Paul come next). Despite this, it is an intriguing text, with some thought-provoking analyses. For example, Hart explains that he ranks Muhammad first because he was the sole founder of Islam, while Jesus and Paul share the responsibility for Christianity. Muhammad was also a great secular leader, while Jesus Christ refused to accept any worldly authority.

What is most pertinent is the author's description of the unique message of Christ. Almost all religions adopt some form of the Golden Rule as a premise, but Jesus was alone in commanding that we forgive enemies, turn the other cheek, or walk a second mile. Hart then quotes the text for this lesson and says that if these words and others from the Sermon on the Mount "were widely followed, I would have no hesitation in placing Jesus first in this book."

There is no legal demand that a human being should love an enemy. In fact, it is difficult for us to love anyone unless we have the security of being loved. Except in a case of sexual infatuation, it's just not logical to expect us to love anyone who doesn't reciprocate our love.

It is even more difficult for us to forgive others if we don't have the assurance of being forgiven. We feel we have to wait, until we are sure that the other person will also forgive us. All of us have probably fallen uncontrollably in love with a potential sweetheart who rejects us. But we don't fall uncontrollably into forgiveness, especially of an enemy! Also, we can love people and not forgive them—a fact proven by the high rate of divorce in our society.

Peter heard the troubling command of Jesus and wanted to ingratiate himself with the Lord—but he also wanted to be sure he didn't go too far. Knowing that some rabbis advocated forgiveness three times, he came to Jesus and asked, "Lord, how often shall my brother sin against me, and I forgive him? until seven times?" Jesus said to him, "I say not to you, 'until seven times,' but 'until seventy times seven' " (Matthew 18:21–22).

Many of us have computed that this is 490 times, but the command is not for me to count patiently if my wife burns toast 490 mornings and then on the 491st time I can finally condemn her! The point of Jesus' teaching is to make forgiveness a permanent attitude, a way of life.

He immediately explained this to Peter with one of his most interesting parables. A servant owed the king 10,000 talents (the modern equivalent is more than $25,000 per talent)—an almost immeasurable debt. The king forgave him, and immediately the servant cast one of his subordinates into prison because he failed to repay a debt of about $15. The other servants reported this to the king, who severely punished the unforgiving one (verses 23–34).

It is somewhat shocking that Jesus says, "Forgive and even love your enemies." Does he mean that we should do this even if we aren't sure that we will be forgiven and loved? Strangely, the answer is no, because forgiveness and love are available to all of us—through Christ. Jesus draws a parallel with us when he adds, "So likewise shall my heavenly Father do unto you, if you from your hearts forgive not every one of his brothers their trespasses" (verse 35).

We have already agreed that it is difficult to love without being loved, and almost impossible to forgive without being forgiven. The teachings of Jesus are predicated on the fact that we receive the unbounded love of God and absolute forgiveness of all our trespasses. Like the king in the parable, God forgives our great debts and expects us to forgive the relatively insignificant grievances we may have against others.

His Healing Touch

C h a p t e r S i x

Jonah and the Big Fish

Now the word of the Lord came to Jonah the son of Amittai, saying, "Arise, go to Nineveh, that great city, and cry against it; for their wickedness has come to me."

But Jonah rose up to flee to Tarshish from the presence of the Lord, and went down to Joppa; and he found a ship going to Tarshish, to go with them to Tarshish from the presence of the Lord.

Jonah 1:1–3

As is the case with "Doubting Thomas" and many other Bible characters, most of us know one thing about Jonah—that a whale (the Bible actually says "big fish") swallowed him. One of the challenges of Bible study is to delve more deeply into a dramatic story and to see how its message might possibly apply to us. Let's take a closer look at this intriguing event.

Nineveh was a city established by Nimrod, son of Cush, son of Ham, son of Noah. It was the massive capital of Assyria, which the prophet Nahum described as "cruel and evil." In the time of Jonah, Nineveh was the ultimate enemy of the Israelites, inhabited by despised Gentiles. It was considered a city condemned by God, with leaders whose equivalents in our day would be a Mu'ammar al-Gadhafi or a Saddam Hussein.

Jonah grew up as a rich kid, welcome even in the royal palace. He was an archconservative, jingoistic supporter of Israelite leaders who were prejudiced against anyone who was not Jewish or might oppose the unrestricted expansion of Judaism. In some commentaries, he has been described in modern language as a klutz or a jerk—one of the most foolish and stubborn biblical characters.

Now let's take another look at this text. God wanted to give the people of Nineveh a chance to repent and be forgiven. How could Jonah betray his own people by traveling to this hated place and delivering such a message? Understandably, this command was abhorrent to Jonah, who wanted the people of Nineveh to be condemned to hell.

Jonah had three options: to obey God, to stay where he was and ignore the command, or to run away and hide. As we know, he chose the third option. Tarshish was at the southern tip of Spain, which was then at the farthest edge of the known world; some people thought that anyone who went farther would fall off the edge and vanish into oblivion. The ships and sailors of Tarshish were known as the finest on the seas.

The ship Jonah was on ran into a great storm and began to founder on the way to its destination, and the crew somehow knew that this was a special tempest sent to punish someone. The sailors cast lots and identified Jonah as the guilty person onboard. They found him asleep in his cabin, and he confessed that he was trying to escape from God. So far as we know, he was the only one on the ship who wasn't praying; he just identified himself as a Hebrew who worshiped "the God of Heaven who made the sea and the dry land."

It's typical of Jonah that he acknowledged the power and omnipresence of God but still refused to pray, repent, or obey. Instead, he finally chose to commit suicide by telling the crew, "Pick me up and throw me into the sea." This they did, the sea was calmed, and Jonah was saved by being taken into a big fish.

Later, Jonah was vomited up on dry land and finally agreed to go to Nineveh. And we note that, despite their sinfulness and rebellion, forgiveness was available both to the people of Nineveh and to Jonah. "So the people of Nineveh believed God, and proclaimed a fast. . . . And God saw their works, that they turned from their evil way; and God repented of the evil that he had said that he would do unto them; and he did it not" (Jonah 3:5, 10). When Jonah saw this, he went into a rage because of God's benevolence, and the story ends, with the fate of the resentful prophet unknown.

The primary lesson of the Book of Jonah is that the Gospel message and the grace and love of God are for all people, not just a few fortunate chosen ones. God is eager to have all people repent and be forgiven. Our own arrogance or prejudice toward others is mistaken and condemned. There are other lessons in this book that compare the all-encompassing mercy and concern we are given by God with the relatively insignificant grievances for which we should be forgiving to our neighbors and loved ones.

For Christians, the words and actions of Jesus provide clear commandments. We should be receptive to them, and we are sadly mistaken if, like Jonah, we think we can escape from the presence of God or the Holy Spirit. This belief separates us from the joy and peace we have been promised.

CHAPTER SEVEN

No More Hiding

When she heard about Jesus, she came up behind him in the crowd and touched his cloak, because she thought, "If I just touch his clothes, I will be healed." Immediately her bleeding stopped and she felt in her body that she was freed from her suffering. . . . [And Jesus] said to her, "Daughter, your faith has healed you. Go in peace and be freed from your suffering."

MARK 5:27–29, 34

There are many healing miracles in the New Testament, but this story from Mark is the only instance I know in which Christ healed someone without taking the initiative or responding deliberately. Frequently, people would come to Jesus—the traveling teacher about whom so many were talking—and say, "I am sick; can you heal me?" But in this case, Jesus did not even know that the healing was taking place until after it had happened, when he realized that power had gone out from him.

By the way, we sometimes assume that Jesus, being God, knew everything; yet in this story, after Jesus becomes aware of the healing, he asks his disciples, "Who touched my clothes?" (verse 30). Clearly Jesus was human enough to have to wonder who touched him when he was jostled in the crowd. It reminds us that he was, in that sense, a person like you or me.

Why did the woman in the story feel the need to sneak up on Jesus rather than ask him directly to heal her? Under the circumstances, it was probably a natural inclination. Remember, first of all, that women were severely oppressed, beginning at birth. When a baby girl was born, neighbors would sometimes wonder, What did those parents do wrong, that they should be given a girl instead of a boy? Economics played a role: a boy was viewed as the future breadwinner of the family, a kind of social security for the future, whereas a girl was considered a burden, someone who couldn't even be married off successfully unless an expensive dowry could be provided. And throughout the life of a girl or a woman, custom would hold her down, restricting her freedom.

So for this suffering woman to come out alone in public was, in itself, probably a difficult thing to do. Furthermore, this woman had a disease that was considered embarrassing or shameful in the Jewish culture of her day. Mark says that she had been subject to bleeding for twelve years. We know that a woman having her monthly period was considered unclean for religious purposes: she could not participate in any sort of religious ceremony or enter the Temple, even its outer porches, and anyone who touched her was considered unclean as well. Imagine the deprivation and loneliness this woman had suffered: for twelve years she had been shunned by other people, forbidden even to go to worship. No wonder she would have been ashamed to make herself known openly. So we can understand the feelings of the suffering woman and her desire to conceal her affliction, even from Jesus.

Many of us have a tendency to conceal our weaknesses, our failures, and our needs. We prefer to demonstrate that we are strong and self-sufficient. This tendency comes out in many ways. In men, it may appear as a macho attitude: "I can stand on my own feet and deal with my own problems. I don't need help, so don't try to help me!" In a business meeting, we may be afraid to admit that we don't know the answer to a question; in a prayer group or Bible study class, we may be embarrassed to confess that we don't understand a passage of Scripture. And when we have a deep personal or spiritual trouble, we may hesitate to seek help from pastors, counselors, or friends, fearing that they will respect us less for admitting we need their guidance.

As a result, we put on disguises—facades to make us appear better, stronger, more self-assured than we really are. And in so doing, we cut ourselves off from other people and from the healing power of God's love, which we can enjoy only if we have the courage to open ourselves to it. Finding that courage begins with facing the truth about ourselves.

A half hour of quiet, sincere contemplation and self-analysis might be the first step. Perhaps we'll want to take a notebook and write down the things we discover about ourselves. "This is what I am, my strengths and weaknesses, the good and the bad in my life so far; and here are the opportunities—and needs—that can bring me closer to God in the future." It's difficult to do this, and to make the commitment to change that it implies, but faith in Jesus and his forgiveness can help.

God doesn't want us to hide our weaknesses and needs but is eager to satisfy them. Remember the end of the story of the bleeding woman: Jesus sought her out in the crowd, told her, "Your faith has healed you," and urged her, "Go in peace." Because she'd found within herself the courage to reach out to Jesus in her need, she was renewed and made whole, not only in body but in spirit, forgiven and freed from her sins, her subterfuge, and her shame.

Christ is ready to do the same for us.

Chapter Eight

She Forgot Her Bucket!

When a Samaritan woman came to draw water, Jesus said to her, "Will you give me a drink?" The Samaritan woman said to him, "You are a Jew and I am a Samaritan woman. How can you ask me for a drink?" (For Jews do not associate with Samaritans.)

Jesus answered her, "If you knew the gift of God and who it is that asks you for a drink, you would have asked him and he would have given you living water." . . .

The woman said to him, "I know the Messiah is coming (He who is called Christ); when that one comes, he will explain all things to us." Jesus said to her, "I who speak to you am he." . . . So the woman left her water pot, and went into the city. . . .

John 4:7–10, 25–26, 28

The encounter between Jesus and the woman at the well is one of the most beloved stories of the New Testament. If you've been to the Middle East, you know that most places are very hot and dry. In Jesus' time, and still today in some places, the women had the job of fetching water from communal wells. It wasn't easy work. In the story John tells, Jesus arrives at the well around noon: about the sixth hour of daylight, as the Bible says. It was unusual to be going to the well at noontime. Most of the women would have drawn their supply of water hours earlier, before the heat of the day.

Why did this particular woman have to go at midday? We can figure out the reason from some of the other things we learn about her. The other women ostracized her because of her promiscuity. "I have no husband," she tells Jesus in verse 17, and he replies, with an insight that amazes her, "The fact is, you have had five husbands, and the man you now have is not your husband" (verse 18). So this was a despised woman, in effect a prostitute, rejected and unforgiven by the people around her.

Imagine the life of such a woman. In the morning, the other women of the neighborhood must have gathered at the well and talked together, shared a joke or two, passed along the latest village gossip, and maybe bragged about their children or grandchildren. Meanwhile, this much-married outcast would have sat in her house, perhaps looking out the window until the others returned home. Only when the road was empty, and she could be sure that she wouldn't be cursed or spat upon, did she dare to slip out of her house to fetch water.

This woman was someone the followers of Jesus would

have condemned and shunned. She was a Samaritan and a whore—both words that would have come like curses from the mouths of many Jews at the time. To ethnic and religious prejudice, we can add the sense of superiority most of us have toward someone we consider immoral.

How did Jesus demonstrate the breaking down of prejudice in his encounter with the Samaritan woman? First, he asked her for a cup of water. No doubt Jesus was thirsty, having been walking on the hot, dusty roads of Samaria all morning. But in asking her to share her water cup, he was very deliberately violating a powerful taboo. It's one that many Americans can understand. It embarrasses me to say it, but I remember well that, when I worked in the peanut fields with my daddy as a young boy, it would have been inconceivable for a white person to drink water from the same dipper as one of the black workers. This was true despite the fact that we were working side by side in the same field and that, on the weekend, I might easily play ball, go fishing, or even sleep with my black friends in their house if my parents were away. Still, the sense of taboo we felt and our prejudice against sharing a cup with a black person were strong and unquestioned.

Jesus shattered a similar prejudice with his matter-of-fact request: Will you give me a drink? It's a simple act, but in the context of his society it's a startling one. From this plain yet revolutionary beginning, the meeting between Jesus and the Samaritan woman goes on to become one of the most remarkable encounters in the Bible. Jesus treats the woman in a way she must have found strange and wonderful. Rather than revile, condemn, or lecture her, Jesus speaks to her with frankness, compassion, and respect. He tells her about his own mission on earth—to become a spring of water welling up to eternal life in the souls of those who believe in him (verse 14). And when the woman expresses her faith that one day a savior called Messiah will come, Jesus confesses, "I who speak to you am he" (verses 25–26).

Amazed and moved by Jesus' understanding of her and by the depth of conviction his words carry, she becomes a follower and a witness for him, and helps to convert many of her fellow Samaritans (verses 39–42). In effect, she takes her place alongside Mary Magdalene as one of the great female disciples of Jesus, who rose from a despised social position to become an inspired witness.

She learned about Jesus Christ, the Messiah, completely forgot her water jug, and ran to the village. Realizing that she was probably considered the most sinful person in the community, she didn't report that she had found the long-awaited Messiah. She only said, "Come and see a man who told me all the things I ever did." And she added a question, "Is not this the Christ?" Then the villagers went to the well to see for themselves, and the Bible says, "And many of the Samaritans of that city believed on him" (verses 29, 39).

She may have lost her bucket, but she gained instead the living water of God's love.

C H A P T E R   N I N E

Where Are You, God?

> Look down from heaven and see from your lofty throne, holy and glorious. Where are your zeal and your might? Your tenderness and compassion are withheld from us. . . . Why, O Lord, do you make us wander from your ways and harden our hearts so we do not revere you? Return for the sake of your servants, the tribes that are your inheritance.
>
> ISAIAH 63:15, 17

Isaiah writes in the so-called postexilic period, when the Jews had returned to Jerusalem after sixty years of captivity under the Persian emperor Cyrus. It was a time much like ours: chaotic, hopeful, and perilous, filled with both opportunities and problems. The Jews were rebuilding the temple, the traditional heart of their faith, but the work was proceeding slowly, and even when it was completed the reconstructed temple would be a far cry from the magnificent edifice Solomon had built, which had been destroyed a generation earlier. Worse still, intermarriage among the Jews and the Canaanites was threatening the Jews' commitment to their faith, and there was a growing sense that the Israelites were a people adrift, lacking in the moral certainty and strength that had sustained them for centuries.

Many Christians today are filled with a similar sense of uneasiness. A number of things seem to be going well in our society: the economy is healthy, democratic principles are on the upswing around the world, and no major military enemy threatens us. Yet in some ways modern life seems increasingly destitute. Crime, violence, greed, drugs, and the dilution of traditional family values are weakening our society's foundations.

Just one statistic: Every day in the United States, seventeen children are killed by gunfire. That's about 6,000 children each year who are killed by guns, as compared, for example, with about 3,000 a year who died at the height of the polio epidemic of the 1950s. We rose up as a society to fight against polio. Why do we not act more forcefully to halt today's even greater scourge? And where is God in all this evil and suffering? These are the kinds of questions that Isaiah asked about his own troubled society more than 2,500 years ago. In the verses quoted here, Isaiah is crying out to God for answers: "Why do you let us abandon your ways? Why do you tolerate evil among us? God, do something!"

The honesty and passion of Isaiah's prayer impress me. It's a cry of anguish, of suffocation, of abandonment, of disappointment. He didn't do what many of us do, which is simply complain about our problems. He approached God directly. Nor did he pray in the superficial, rote manner we often adopt—reciting a few traditional words for perhaps sixty seconds a day. He leveled with God in an intensely personal way.

My sister Ruth had a habit of praying as though she was talking to a friend about the constantly evolving events of her life. She always seemed to be aware of the presence of the Holy Spirit and could communicate easily and with complete confidence. It was disconcerting that, despite our sincere attempts, she was never able to impart to me such a highly personal and intimate relationship with Christ. My prayers are usually more formal, as I speak somewhat cautiously to Almighty God.

Let's imagine that we've become alienated from our closest friend, someone we've known and loved and with whom we've shared life for many years. Maybe one of us has said or done something cruel or thoughtless to hurt the other; perhaps we've allowed the faithless act to make us grow apart, so that we haven't spoken for months. Yet all the while, we've longed to be reunited in the old love that meant so much to us both.

Now, imagine further that we have just a short time—ten minutes, say—to see our friend and be reconciled. What would the conversation be like? Would it be superficial, formal, and polite? No, it would more likely be a cry from the heart. That's what Isaiah's prayer to God is like. "God, where are you?" he cries. "Come back to me, let me see you! We are your children, the ones you chose to love. Open up the heavens and help us!"

It's rare for us to pray with such perfect frankness. Even in our most private thoughts, we like to conceal who we really are. We don't want God to see our selfishness, our inadequacy, our weakness. But Isaiah got to the heart of things. Seeing God's people floundering in sin and alienation from God, he expressed their anguish fully and freely.

And what is God's answer to Isaiah's painful questions? In the prophet's day and in our own the answer is the same, one that, perhaps, we know in our hearts. Though we cry out, "Where is God?" it's not God who is lost—it is we. As human beings have always done, we wander away from the presence of God and find ourselves suddenly alone. But we are the ones who have left the right road; God has not abandoned us.

Where is God? God is here, in you and me. In the Book of Revelation, Jesus says, "Here I am! I stand at the door and knock. If anyone hears my voice and opens the door, I will come in and eat with him, and he with me" (3:20). We are always in the presence of the Holy Spirit, as my sister Ruth seemed to know. Whether the door is open or closed is our decision.

CHAPTER TEN

The Cost of Grace

We then, as workers together with him, beseech you also that ye receive not the grace of God in vain. . . .

For ye know the grace of our Lord Jesus Christ, that, though he was rich, yet for your sakes he became poor, that ye through his poverty might be rich.

2 CORINTHIANS 6:1, 8:9

As followers of Jesus Christ, we must realize that grace—the free gift of God—is not free. Someone has spelled out *grace* as God's Riches At Christ's Expense, and the phrase isn't just beautiful but very apt. We have seen that the early disciples of Jesus were eager to face severe deprivation or punishment as they proudly exhibited their faith.

In our own era, one of the best examples of this lesson is the great German theologian Dietrich Bonhoeffer. He was a Protestant pastor during Hitler's Nazi regime, leading churches not only in Germany but in Spain and England as well. A good friend of Reinhold Niebuhr, another eminent German theologian who had moved to the United States, Bonhoeffer was lecturing in America at Niebuhr's invitation when Hitler attained power in Germany.

Niebuhr urged Bonhoeffer to remain in America, for his own safety. Bonhoeffer refused. He felt he had to be among the other Christians who he knew were being persecuted in Germany. So he returned home, and for the rest of his life he played a role in the resistance to Hitler. He preached publicly against Nazism, racism, and anti-Semitism. And he kept secret the plot to assassinate Hitler, which one of Bonhoeffer's relatives helped to organize in 1944. Naturally, each of these acts put his life at risk.

Bonhoeffer was finally arrested and imprisoned, and in 1945, just a few days before the allied armies liberated Germany, he was executed on the orders of Heinrich Himmler. He died a disciple and a martyr. His life, we can see, was a modern parallel to the martyrdom suffered by many of the earliest Christians. One of Bonhoeffer's most famous books is titled *The Cost of Discipleship*. Although he wrote this book several years before his execution, the cost of Bonhoeffer's own faith is obvious: he paid the greatest earthly price, his life. Yet Bonhoeffer's message is that, for all of us, there is no such thing as cheap grace.

Personally, I find this message especially challenging: that it's never easy to follow Christ with a full commitment. The temptation—a powerful one—is always there to temper our acts, to modify our commitment, to equivocate or make excuses when we are called upon to do something challenging, painful, or sacrificial on behalf of Christ. We don't want to seem naïve or foolish. To live up to our faith in every moment of our lives is impossible for us as human beings.

For most of us it costs nothing to preach, to speak about our Christian beliefs, to attend church services, or to say, "I'm a Christian." But there's another element to our Christianity. We need to ask ourselves, "What have I actually done that proves my loyalty to Christ? How many times have I sacrificed my own well-being for that of others, in the name of Christ—this week, this month, or even during the last five years?"

Fortunately, the same Holy Spirit that energized and encouraged the first disciples, and that gave Dietrich Bonhoeffer the strength to stand up against Nazi tyranny, is available to us today, wherever and however we live. And if we ask for the help of that Spirit, we will receive it.

Chapter Eleven

The Good Shepherd

I am the good shepherd. The good shepherd lays down his life for the sheep. The hired hand is not the shepherd who owns the sheep. So when he sees the wolf coming, he abandons the sheep and runs away. Then the wolf attacks the flock and scatters it. The man runs away because he is a hired hand and cares nothing for the sheep.

John 10:11–13

Rosalynn and I have visited China a number of times, and as a result I feel very close to the Chinese people. As president, I decided that the United States would normalize diplomatic relations with China, and when this was done in January 1979 the late premier Deng Xiaoping visited the White House. He explained to me the changes he planned for China. At that time the communal farms were all owned by the state and were worked together by the local farmers.

By 1981, when we made a return visit to China, Deng had permitted each farm family to have the crop from 15 percent of the land, and he'd also allowed each farmer—but no urban families—to start one small industry. They could make clay pots, repair bicycles, raise a few mink, and so on. This was the start of the capitalist-style industry now exploding throughout China. In explaining his plan, Deng made an interesting observation: that no Chinese farmer would stay up all night with a sick hog if it belonged to the state farm, but if it was his own animal, he'd tend it until morning to make sure it survived. That's human nature, he said, and he admitted that he'd probably act the same way.

It's also the image Jesus is drawing in these verses, to describe his love for us. He is the good shepherd, who lays down his life for the sheep, rather than the mere hired hand, who flees when danger comes near.

Of course, it's not very flattering for us to be compared to sheep! When I grew up, we always had a flock of sheep on our farm, and we considered them dumb and meek. They look big, but most of their size comes from their fluffy wool, and they appeared pitiful and even a little ugly after we sheared the wool. When attacked, sheep are utterly unable to defend themselves. Stray dogs were the main predators that concerned us. It seemed that once a dog killed sheep for food, he would later do so even when he wasn't hungry, almost as an addiction—because they were so vulnerable and helpless. Such a dog had to be destroyed.

So calling us sheep is not very flattering, but in using the imagery of sheep and shepherd to describe God's relationship to humans, Jesus was drawing on a wealth of biblical tradition. Maybe the most beloved chapter in the Bible is the Twenty-third Psalm, the beautiful poem that begins, "The Lord is my shepherd, I shall not want. He makes me lie down in green pastures." Pastors report that this is the Bible passage most requested by people who are seriously ill or overcome with grief. The presence of God as a guardian and comforter in our lives is something we desperately hunger to believe, and this psalm expresses that faith magnificently. We Americans, being especially proud of our independence, willpower, and self-sufficiency, may not like to think of ourselves as followers, but there's nothing wrong with being subservient if Christ is our leader.

The truth is, we're all vulnerable, not only to danger and misfortune but also to temptation, fear, doubt, and selfishness. We're vulnerable, like sheep, to being led astray; we're vulnerable to forces that can destroy our lives, turning us away from our families, friends, and neighbors. And the superficial trappings we hope will protect us—possessions, reputation, pride—do no more to make us secure than the sheep's fluffy wool. Just below the surface, we're helpless and in need of Christ's guidance and protection.

And when we think of sheep in a biblical context, we should also remember the special use of the image of a sheep in Isaiah's description of the suffering servant: "We all, like sheep, have gone astray, each of us has turned to his own way; and the Lord has laid on him the iniquity of us all. He was oppressed and afflicted, yet he did not open his mouth; he was led like a lamb to the slaughter, and as a sheep before her shearers is silent, so he did not open his mouth" (53:6–7).

Christians, of course, read Isaiah's description as a prophecy of Christ: the savior who took upon himself the iniquity of us all, suffering in silence on our behalf. How vividly the words evoke the last hours of Jesus and his willing, unprotesting death at the hands of his enemies!

The imagery seems paradoxical. Isaiah is describing the ruler of the universe, the Savior and Messiah, in the form of a sheep, vulnerable and helpless. But the nature of Christ is equally paradoxical: victim and redeemer, servant and ruler, man and God.

The vulnerability and foolishness of a sheep may not be characteristics we're eager to confess we have. We may prefer to imagine that we are strong and able to take care of ourselves. But that belief is an illusion, as the troubles and failures of our lives show us. Fortunately, in Jesus we have a shepherd whom we can trust with our weakness and helplessness. He took our vulnerability upon himself and laid down his life for us, only to rise again in triumph. Now he offers us hope, reassurance, and security as part of his wandering but ever-loved flock.

Who Is My Neighbor?

Chapter Twelve

I Will Be with You

> But now, this is what the Lord says: "Fear not, for I have redeemed you; I have called you by name; you are mine.
> "When you pass through the waters, I will be with you."
>
> Isaiah 43:1–2

The presence of another person can be a transforming experience in our lives. At times, it can mean the difference between life and death. Something most parents know, which physicians have now proven, is that a baby has an innate need, a hunger, for the loving presence of an adult. If a baby is not touched and held, it will not grow and mature properly.

At Grady Hospital in Atlanta, we see vividly what this means. Many premature babies are born there, and some of their mothers are addicted to crack cocaine. In fact, more than 15 percent of the babies are addicted to cocaine at birth. All too often, their mothers are incapable of caring for them properly. These babies would languish without proper nurturing; some would even die. Fortunately, there are a lot of volunteers who go to Grady and do nothing more than sit and hold them. It makes all the difference in the world to the babies; it makes them feel well and strong, and it teaches them to respond to other people. And the volunteers tell me it's one of the most gratifying times of their week.

Not only babies have this deep need for contact with other human beings. My mother, whom everyone called Miss Lillian, was a registered nurse who volunteered to go into the Peace Corps at the age of sixty-eight. She was sent to India, where she served in a small village near Bombay, working in a clinic. The people she cared for were terribly poor; many of them didn't have enough to eat, and they lacked access to proper health care, education, and good jobs. What made their plight worse was that some of them suffered from terrible diseases, including leprosy, which made others shun them.

We know from the Bible that the people of Jesus' time also shunned those suffering from leprosy. There was a common belief that God was punishing lepers for their sins, or perhaps the sins of their parents. So nobody would go near them, not only because of the risk of contagion but because lepers were considered inferior, even subhuman. (Think of how we sometimes treat people suffering from AIDS today. This helps us understand the significance of Jesus' example.)

Jesus Christ broke down this barrier, as he broke down so many others. He reached out to the lepers, curing many and comforting all, and teaching us a lesson in the importance of sharing our presence even with people who are despised or rejected by others.

During her time in India, my mother discovered the truth of that lesson. But she learned it the hard way, as described in one of my poems.

MISS LILLIAN SEES LEPROSY FOR THE FIRST TIME

When I nursed in a clinic near Bombay,
a small girl, shielding all her leprous sores,
crept inside the door. I moved away,
but then the doctor said, "You take this case!"
First I found a mask and put it on,
quickly gave the child a shot and then,
not well, I slipped away to be alone
and scrubbed my entire body red and raw.

I faced her treatment every week with dread
and loathing for the chore, not the child.
As time passed, I was less afraid,
and managed not to turn my face away.
Her spirit bloomed as sores began to fade.
She'd raise her anxious, searching eyes to mine,
to show she trusted me. We'd smile and say
a few Marathi words, then reach and hold
each other's hands. And then love grew between
us, so that when I kissed her lips
I didn't feel unclean.

After this, my mother spent much of her time with people suffering from leprosy and through her nursing skills was able to bring relief to some of them, helping to cure the sores on their bodies and restore their strength. Perhaps her patients had the same needs as the babies at Grady. And what Mama found was that she received from the experience as much as she gave. When she held the hand of a leprous girl, gave a poor villager some food delicacies we had sent her from home, or used the few dollars in pay she received from the Peace Corps to buy medicine for the clinic, she found her own life transformed in a wonderful way. After her return from India, Mama traveled around the country giving humorous but emotional lectures about her experiences and encouraging her audiences not to let advancing age or anything else prevent them from reaching out to others.

God's promise to the Israelites is a promise we all need to hear: "I love you, and I will be with you, no matter what happens." The presence of one who cares for us is a healing, nurturing gift. And when we give our presence to another person, especially one who is lonely, needy, or outcast, the blessing returns to us.

CHAPTER THIRTEEN

Knowing and Being Known

When Jesus saw Nathanael approaching, he said of him, "Here is a true Israelite, in whom there is nothing false." "How do you know me?" Nathanael asked.

Jesus answered, "I saw you while you were still under the fig tree before Philip called you."

Then Nathanael declared, "Rabbi, you are the Son of God; you are the King of Israel."

JOHN 1:47–49

The Gospel of John has a unique role in the New Testament. The other three Gospels, often called "synoptic," have much in common: they tell many of the same stories, often using the same words, and they follow similar outlines of Jesus' life. In fact, most biblical scholars believe that the synoptic Gospels are all based on the same source, which may be either the Gospel of Mark or some undiscovered document from which Matthew, Mark, and Luke all borrowed.

John's Gospel is quite different from the others in tone and style, as well as in many of the details of Jesus' life. One of the most significant differences is that, for John, the divine nature of Jesus is present and apparent from the very beginning of the story, whereas for the other evangelists, it becomes obvious only gradually. John's Gospel begins with the beautiful verses "In the beginning was the Word, and the Word was with God, and the Word was God. He was with God in the beginning. Through him all things were made; without him nothing was made that has been made" (1:1–3). The theological meaning of these verses is complex and profound, but their central message is that Jesus' divine nature not only predates his life on earth but predates the very beginning of time itself.

Most Christians are familiar with the biblical scene in which Peter responds to Jesus' question "Who do you say I am?" with the words "You are the Christ, the Son of the living God" (Matthew 16:16). We tend to think of this as the first time that any of Jesus' followers knew that he was the Son of God. We're inclined to forget that Nathanael, quite early in the earthly ministry of Jesus, says to him, "You are the Son of God." This exclamation reminds us that, for John, Jesus' divinity is clear from the beginning.

How did Nathanael perceive so quickly that Jesus was the Christ? Was he given some kind of revelation? We don't know. But John's account suggests that Nathanael knew because of the simple statement "I saw you while you were still under the fig tree before Philip called you."

It's a curious scene; perhaps if I had been Nathanael, I would have looked for some natural explanation for Jesus' words. Maybe, in the moments before Philip called Nathanael, Jesus had followed Philip and had seen Nathanael from afar, perhaps by standing on a hillside or behind a large stone. Yet Nathanael did not consider this possibility. He reacted to Jesus' words as if being seen under a fig tree had some special meaning for him.

This may be the case. The King James Bible refers to figs or fig trees forty-one times in thirty-nine different verses, several of which describe the fig tree as a place of worship. For the ancient Jews, it seems, the shade of a fig tree was a special location one might seek if one wanted to be secluded for a few moments of intense prayer. Maybe Nathanael was praying under the fig tree when Philip approached him; we don't know. This was a momentous event, almost miraculous: that Jesus and Nathanael knew each other intimately, and almost instantaneously.

In our lives, knowing others and being known are experiences of great psychological and spiritual significance. In fact, the two really go together. "Know thyself" was the motto of the Greek philosophers; but how do we get to know ourselves? Is it simply by looking inward? More often, I think, we come to know ourselves through our relationships with others. As we interact with the people around us, we find reflected back to us the characteristics we reveal to them. By the ways in which they respond to us, we can see how we appear and what sort of impression we make upon them. As we grow up, our self-images—and character—are largely shaped by our encounters with those around us.

Naturally, in most of our relationships we try hard to

control how we appear. We're usually eager to reveal only our better sides. Rather than show qualities like selfishness, pride, or weakness, we work at appearing generous, modest, and strong. This desire to impress people favorably is, in moderation, a good thing. We are better people because we are concerned about others' opinions of us.

But in our most intimate relationships—with a spouse, a close friend, or anyone with whom we feel really comfortable—we are more likely to reveal our true selves. In a perfect friendship, we can be truly intimate because we trust the other person to accept and forgive our flaws, failings, and weaknesses. And if we can do the same for the other, then a richly rewarding relationship of increasing mutual knowledge and self-improvement is possible. A person who is unwilling or unable to enter into such an intimate relationship loses one of the great opportunities in life.

As for Nathanael with Jesus, there is something special in any relationship where we feel known and understood from the very beginning, as if we've known each other for years. We marvel, because such a relationship is rare and precious; not everyone is lucky enough ever to experience it.

But for all of us, a friendship of this kind is available with Jesus Christ. Just as he knew Nathanael from the beginning, Jesus has always known us. His understanding and his love for us are perfect and absolute. We can share with him the truth about ourselves, both good and bad, in the certain knowledge that he will forgive—has forgiven—our every sin and flaw, and can guide us to a better life.

CHAPTER FOURTEEN

The Jealousy Trap

When the men were returning home after David had killed the Philistine, the women came out from all the towns of Israel to meet King Saul with singing and dancing, with joyful songs and with tambourines and lutes. As they danced, they sang: "Saul has slain his thousands, and David his tens of thousands."

Saul was very angry; this refrain galled him. "They have credited David with tens of thousands," he thought, "but me with only thousands. What more can he get but the kingdom?" And from that time on Saul kept a jealous eye on David.

1 SAMUEL 18:6–9

Saul, Israel's first king, ruled the nation at the time of their war against the Philistines. And although God had anointed

Saul as king, he had turned away from God's commandments, becoming proud, arrogant, and disobedient. By the time David killed Goliath, the champion of the Philistines, we are told that the Spirit of the Lord had departed from Saul (1 Samuel 16:14), so, although he was still sovereign, his self-confidence and his hold on power were increasingly insecure.

Thus, we can understand all too well his reaction to the triumphal greeting that David receives when he returns home after killing Goliath. In David, Saul sees a potential rival, someone whose popularity and heroism have won him the acclaim of the Israelites and may, Saul fears, win the throne as well.

But notice the effect that Saul's jealousy has upon him. First of all, it blinds him to David's true nature. David has no ambition to replace Saul; he is interested simply in serving his king, his nation, and his God. Through all the rest of Saul's life, as we learn from the later chapters of the first book of Samuel, he will seek David's death, driven by his jealousy; yet David will remain loyal to Saul. This will still be true even at the end of Saul's life, when the king meets his death at the hands of his own armor bearer, whom Saul has begged to kill him. David punishes the armor bearer with death, declaring that in striking down Saul he has killed the Lord's anointed. David's behavior is one of the most remarkable demonstrations of loyalty and humility anywhere in the Bible. Yet Saul, driven nearly insane by jealousy, is unable to recognize it.

Notice, too, how Saul's jealousy destroys joy in his own accomplishments. Saul is the undisputed leader, and the victories of his army, including the deeds of David, are ultimately to Saul's credit. Yet Saul is unable to celebrate them. His triumphs bring him no pleasure because he perceives David's as greater.

Finally, Saul's jealousy gradually erodes the remnants of virtue in his character. In the latter portions of chapter 18, we see Saul engaging in ever-greater acts of treachery toward David. He promises each of his daughters in marriage, not intending to keep his word but hoping that David will be killed by the Philistines before the wedding can take place. When these plots fail, he simply orders his son Jonathan to murder David; this, too, fails. Throughout, Saul's jealousy and fear feed each other. When Saul realized that the Lord was with David, we are told, he became still more afraid of him (18:28–29).

What role does jealousy play in our lives? Our society is so largely based on competition—in business, in schools, in sports, in the arts, in politics—that jealousy is difficult to escape. Think about the situations that provoke feelings of envy in us. Maybe it's when we meet a high school or college classmate who has become very successful; perhaps it's when a competitor in our business or profession wins a big contract or makes a lot of money. Maybe it's when a person that we don't much like builds a house nearby that's nicer than ours, or raises a child—or even worse, a grandchild—who is more successful than ours! Our innermost hearts can tell us what pushes our personal jealousy buttons.

Almost all of us are prone to jealousy; I'm no exception. I'll admit, I'm inclined to envy the accomplishments of my successors in public office and to resent their sometimes blaming problems on me. "Nothing succeeds like successors," as some wit once said. But jealousy is a trait I struggle to overcome.

When jealousy is left unchecked, its effects on our character can be devastating. It makes us want to drag down others who've achieved something rather than celebrate their accomplishments. So we look for opportunities to talk about their small flaws, failings, or sins; we join the rumor mill and share negative gossip every chance we get. And the more we do this, the more mean and petty we become, and the more pleasure in our own good things is spoiled.

How can we escape the downward spiral of jealousy that helped to destroy Saul? One key is to reexamine our standards of success. Remember that as Christians we've pledged to pattern our lives after Jesus. The real measures of success are the things that he said were important—in the words of St. Paul, the things we cannot see, like truth, compassion, justice, service, and love.

Another key, perhaps more difficult, is to develop a genuine sense of friendship toward our neighbors, so that we can relish their achievements. This is the same feeling we would normally have, for instance, about our own children.

Rather than asking, "How can I increase my income to surpass that of my neighbor?" or "How can I get a better job than my classmate at college?" try asking, "What can I do to make my life more significant in the eyes of my Savior, Jesus Christ?" If we can reorient our lives to make this our focus, then we can be freed, little by little, from the burning desire to excel our neighbors in the realms of power, wealth, and prestige. Instead, we may find that we are able to admire and share the joys and achievements of those around us, to boost them up rather than tear them down. That's a liberation more gratifying, exciting, and permanent than any worldly success.

CHAPTER FIFTEEN

The Art of Forgiving

Do not judge, and you will not be judged. Do not condemn, and you will not be condemned. Forgive, and you will be forgiven.

LUKE 6:37

One of the most difficult challenges in life is truly to forgive someone who has injured us. In some cases, the passage of time can help. As the years go by, the pain we suffered grows less, and so does our resentment, until one day we discover that our anger and bitterness are almost or completely gone. We may not even remember the original dispute.

In other cases, however, the anger grows. This may be particularly likely in instances where our paths repeatedly cross those of the people who hurt us. It's easy to find ourselves selectively noticing everything hateful or despicable about the other people and ignoring all they do that is admirable or generous, so that our feeling of condemnation increases with the years. In the most extreme case, we can become obsessed with someone else whom we blame for blighting our life. The result can be an existence mired in bitterness and despair.

As Christians, we have a special responsibility to avoid letting resentment of others fester in us. Jesus specifically commands us to forgive our neighbors—and not just once or twice, or even seven times, but seventy times seven (Matthew 18:22). Furthermore, the Scriptures repeatedly state or imply that unless we are willing to forgive others, we ourselves will not be forgiven—not only by our fellow human beings but by God.

We're warned, then, that our resentment of others constitutes a barrier, not only between ourselves and them but between us and God. It's a danger that Christians need to take seriously. This was brought home to me years ago, during my 1966 campaign for governor of Georgia. While on a political tour of the Georgia coast, I made plans to attend Sunday morning services at an old Episcopal church on St. Simons Island with Philip Alston, a good friend. I was surprised when he called me at the last minute to explain that he couldn't receive holy communion that Sunday because he felt unable to forgive someone who had slighted him.

At first I thought he was foolish, but soon I realized that Philip's scruples were biblically based. In his Sermon on the Mount, Jesus warns us, "If you are offering your gift at the altar and there remember that your brother has something against you, leave your gift there in front of the altar. First go and be reconciled to your brother, then come and offer your gift" (Matthew 5:23).

To forgive and to be forgiven, then, are reciprocal acts. We can't have one without the other. But to forgive another who has seriously wronged us is not easy. Anger has a way of springing back to life inside us, even when we feel we have laid it aside for good. Perhaps Jesus' admonition to forgive our brother seventy times seven times refers to the fact that we may have to overcome our own inner anger in reaction to a single offense that many times! Sometimes the only way to put aside our resentment is deliberately to take an overt step toward reconciliation—difficult though it may be.

One of the most important events in my political life was the debate between then-governor Ronald Reagan and me during the 1980 presidential campaign. Sometime afterward we learned that a copy of my secret, personal briefing book for that debate had been stolen beforehand by a Reagan supporter who worked for me in the White House. Eventually, it became known that a noted columnist and author had used the purloined briefing book to help prepare my opponent for the debate. My positions on all the important issues, my analyses of Reagan's positions, my assessment of his vulnerabilities, my tactical plans for the debate, the words and phrases I hoped to use for verbal parries and responses—all of these were known and used against me by a respected journalist who professed fairness and objectivity.

Obviously, I think that what he did was very wrong. But, to my detriment, I retained the resentment for years after the event. Try as I might, I could not bring myself to forgive him until one day, as I was preparing a Sunday School lesson on this very topic of forgiveness, my own hypocrisy was too much to ignore. I decided to think of some concrete step I could take to break down the barrier of anger I'd allowed to grow between the columnist and myself. Casting about for something—anything—that he and I had in common, I finally thought of books we'd written.

My family and I have long been avid baseball fans, and I knew that he had written a book on the subject. I'd avoided reading it, but now I visited a used bookshop near The Carter Center in Atlanta and bought an old copy for a dollar.

I had to admit it was a good book. After reading it, I wrote the author a note, telling him how I had bought his book, expressing my appreciation for the insights he had given me into some of the intricacies of baseball, and offering reconciliation after our long feud. He responded in good humor, only regretting that I hadn't bought a new copy of his book at the full price! Now, much to my relief, I can read his column or see him offering his opinions on television with a much more positive reaction than before. At least partially, one of my resentments has been removed.

Is there a burden of anger, hurt, or resentment toward someone weighing upon us? We shouldn't ignore it any longer. With God's help, we can think of some gesture of forgiveness and reconciliation to offer, and have the courage to make the first move. Doing so can be an important step toward emotional and psychological healing and a new freedom in the grace of Christ's love.

CHAPTER SIXTEEN

The Least of These

Jesus said, "A certain man was going down from Jerusalem to Jericho; and he fell among robbers, and they stripped him and beat him, and went off leaving him half dead. And a certain priest was going down on that road, and when he saw him, he passed by on the other side. And a Levite also, when he came to the place and saw him, passed by on the other side. But a certain Samaritan, who was on a journey, came upon him, and when he saw him, he felt compassion. . . . Which of these three do you think proved to be a neighbor to the man who was robbed?"

LUKE 10:30–33, 36

> And as Jesus entered a certain village, ten leprous men . . . said, "Jesus, Master, have mercy on us!" And . . . they were cleansed. Now one of them . . . fell on his face at His feet, giving thanks to Him. And he was a Samaritan. And Jesus said, "Was no one found who turned back to give glory to God, except this foreigner?"
>
> LUKE 17:12–18

> So he came to Sychar, a city of Samaria, and Jacob's well was there. Jesus therefore, being wearied from his journey, was sitting thus by the well. It was about the sixth hour. And there came a woman of Samaria to draw water. Jesus said to her, "Give me a drink."
>
> JOHN 4:5–7

In 1976, I was invited to speak to the 17,000 delegates assembled for the Southern Baptist Convention. Later that year, I would be elected U.S. president, but I was asked to speak because I was an active member of the Brotherhood Commission, not because of my political status. Three of us were asked to represent Baptist men, and we were requested to limit our speeches to five minutes each.

I was very concerned when I looked at the program, because the first speaker was the eloquent and charismatic Billy Graham, and I had to follow him. And then I was somewhat relieved, because the person speaking after me was a truck driver. I was told that he was literate, but not well educated, and I thought to myself, "Well, I suppose that at least I'll sound good compared with him."

As we sat on the stage waiting to be introduced, the truck driver told me he had never made a speech in his life. "I don't think I can live through it," he said. "I just can't do it." He was drenched with sweat, and I was barely able to prevent his fleeing. Billy Graham gave one of his usual forceful and inspirational talks, and I did the best I could with my own remarks.

Then the truck driver got up, and for a long time he just stood there. Someone took him a glass of water, and he almost mumbled into the microphone, "I was always drunk, and didn't have any friends. The only people I knew were men like me who hung around the bars in the town where I lived." Then someone—he didn't remember who—told him about Christ, and he wanted to tell other people. He studied the Bible, and talked to some men in the local church where he became a member. The only places he felt at ease were barrooms, and he began to talk to customers there. The bartender told him he was ruining his business and should find some other place to make a nuisance of himself.

But he persisted, and eventually the folks in the bar looked forward to asking him questions. He said, "At first they treated me like a joke, but I kept up with the questions and when I couldn't answer one, I went and got the answer and came back with it. Fourteen of my friends became Christians." He stood there a few seconds, and then returned to his seat.

The truck driver's speech, of course, was the highlight of the convention. I don't believe anyone who was there will ever forget that five-minute fumbling statement—or remember what I or even Billy Graham had to say.

Shortly before I taught this lesson in Washington, Rosalynn and I had been to the play *Man of La Mancha*, in which the archidealist Don Quixote falls in love with a prostitute. He calls her Dulcinea, and she spits on him and makes fun of him. Later, as he lies on his deathbed, she reappears and we discover that her life has been transformed. This old, foolish man had had confidence in her—much more than she thought she deserved. He had exalted her out of her absolute sinfulness, and her life was changed.

Now let's look at the Samaritans. Rosalynn and I visited Israel in 1983 and went to Mount Gerazim, which is traditionally viewed as their holy place and center of worship, much as the Jews viewed the city of Jerusalem. We met some Samaritans there, among about 600 Samaritans still left at that time. I don't know how many there are now.

In New Testament times, the Samaritans were a half-Jewish group, related to yet separate from the mainstream Jewish community. Descended from Abraham, Isaac, and Jacob, the Samaritans worshiped God, although they accepted only the first five books of the Hebrew Scriptures—the Torah, or Pentateuch, as it is sometimes called—as authoritative. They'd settled in Samaria at the time that the Jews were permitted by the Assyrian Empire to return to Israel and, rejecting the preaching of Ezra, many Samaritans intermarried with members of other local tribes. In time they came to be regarded as half-breeds, Jews who had betrayed their people and their faith by intermarriage.

At the time of Jesus, the Samaritans were generally despised by mainstream Jews and were forbidden to worship in the Temple at Jerusalem (even if they'd wanted to). They were considered unclean, physically and spiritually. Even to set foot in Samaria was thought improper by many Jews.

The Scriptures quoted at the beginning of this lesson are the only three occasions when Jesus is known to have dealt with Samaritans. In every case, they turn out to be heroes.

The context for Jesus' stories about the Samaritans, then, is a highly prejudiced, sharply divided society—one not unlike our own. To understand the attitude, just think about how many Americans feel about the very poor, about people of color, about certain immigrant groups, or about people of different faiths. For Samaritan, substitute black, Muslim, AIDS victim, Haitian—or perhaps roll them all into one! For Jesus to speak with a Samaritan—and a Samaritan whore, to boot—was a bold blow against deeply ingrained prejudice. His acknowledging the gratitude of the healed leper and using a Samaritan's actions as epitomizing the Golden Rule are powerful lessons against prejudice.

Like those of the alcoholic truck driver and Dulcinea, the lives of the Samaritan woman and the leper were transformed when someone was interested in and cared for them. There are always barriers between us and people who are different, lonely, or in need, and it is natural and convenient for us to refrain from crossing those lines. One of the greatest fears is of being embarrassed—of being publicly scorned or rejected, or of getting ourselves out on a limb and having it chopped off. But who builds and maintains the barriers? We do.

We have the same mandate about witnessing to others that Jesus gave his disciples when they rejoined him at the Samaritan well: "Behold, I say unto you, 'Lift up your eyes, and look on the fields; for they are white already to harvest' " (verse 35). But some of us will live out the rest of our lives—ten, twenty, thirty years—and never attempt to break through the obstacles that separate us from those who may be eager to have a new friend, or to learn about Jesus Christ, our Savior.

The truth is that we are too comfortable with our prejudices. They become so deeply ingrained that we're scarcely aware of them. We can go on happily for a lifetime, barely aware of the thoughts, needs, and talents of others who look, sound, and behave differently from us. But that's not the way of life Jesus intends for us. By his own example, Jesus shows us how to overcome the barriers that separate us from other people, and the amazing ways our lives can be enriched when we dare to take the first step toward an "unattractive" person.

CHAPTER SEVENTEEN

Who Among Us Is Superior?

> The other disciples therefore said to Thomas, "We have seen the Lord." But he said to them, "Unless I shall see in his hands the print of the nails, and put my finger into the print of the nails, and thrust my hand into his side, I will not believe."
>
> JOHN 20:25

After Jesus was crucified, the disciples were afraid for their own lives, and there is little doubt that they were also blaming each other for the tragedy that had occurred. They hadn't even stayed awake when Jesus was in distress and praying in the Garden of Gethsemane, and no one had come forward to testify for him during his trial before the Sanhedrin. All were guilty of abandoning him, but they were undoubtedly arranging others in degrees of guilt, with Judas at the top, perhaps Peter second because he had denied Christ, all the way down the line. It was natural for each to seek some justification for his own actions.

There was a new scapegoat when Christ appeared, and Thomas, who was absent, later refused to believe that the Lord was risen. Down through the ages, Peter's name has become exalted, while his compatriot has been stigmatized by the epithet Doubting Thomas. We are inclined to ascribe an inferior status to Thomas because of his lack of faith.

It is human nature to arrange other people in some kind of order, based on our personal observations or prejudices. Somewhere on the list we insert ourselves, perhaps in a somewhat exalted position. Jesus warns us against doing this, in a stern manner: "Judge not, that you be not judged" (Matthew 7:1).

The habit of judging and ranking people applies across societies, nations, and ethnic groups. I hear ostensibly enlightened and humanitarian people deriding Africans as lacking ambition, intelligence, and ability—much as we used to hear during segregation days from racists about our black neighbors. We at The Carter Center have had the opportunity to know and work with countless Africans, and we see the reality behind the stereotypes. We have helped with an agricultural project that we call Global 2000, mostly financed by a Japanese foundation and guided by Nobel Laureate Norman Borlaug, a noted agronomist and the father of the "green revolution" in India and Pakistan during the late 1960s. After I conclude an agreement with the leader of each nation in the project, we provide the country with one scientist, who trains several hundred native extension workers. They ride bicycles from one small farm to another, teaching and supervising the planting, cultivating, and harvesting practices of the local farmers. The average farm size is only about two acres.

The program is amazingly successful throughout Africa—primarily because these "backward" families are intelligent, competent, and as eager to succeed as anyone we've ever known. In most cases, we are able to increase their production of corn, wheat, sorghum, and millet threefold, using primitive implements, the right varieties of seed, moderate applications of fertilizer, planting in contour rows, and harvesting at the right time. We now have about 600,000 families in twelve African nations participating in this program.

Our most notable success has been in Ethiopia, where abject starvation in 1986 precipitated the global Live Aid concert. When we began our Global 2000 program in 1993, Ethiopia was producing 5.5 million tons of grain for its 60 million people—still a starvation diet. In 1996, the nation's grain yield was 11.7 million tons! In January 1997, its leaders were proud to announce that they were exporting surplus corn to adjacent nations and would be self-sufficient in wheat in 1997. That's what Africans can do!

Now let's take another look at Thomas. When Jesus decided to go to Bethany to console Mary and Martha because their brother Lazarus had died, everyone knew that this was a time of extreme danger. Jesus had already warned his disciples about the cruel fate that awaited him. Listen to the courageous reaction of the same disciple we often disparage: "Then said Thomas, which is called Didymus, unto his fellow disciples, 'Let us also go, that we may die with him' " (John 11:16).

It's significant to see what happened eight days after Jesus' resurrection, when he appeared again to the disciples, this time with Thomas present. There was no cataclysmic event.

Jesus just said, "Peace be unto you," and to Thomas, "Reach here your finger, and behold my hands; and reach here your hand, and thrust it into my side: and be not faithless, but believing." And Thomas then said to him, "My Lord and my God!" (John 20:26–28).

It is surprising that Thomas is the only person in the Bible ever to call Jesus "God." The disciple we stigmatize as the "doubter" had an especially insightful faith. So Thomas is not all that bad, not any worse than the rest of the disciples—or us. All of us doubt; all of us sin; all of us sometimes forget how much Jesus loves us.

It's clear that everyone is different, we sometimes react in strange ways, and we can never fully understand one another. But we know that Christ understands us and forgives our mistakes, and his love is unshakable. He teaches us to do the same: "Judge not . . ."

What We Believe

Chapter Eighteen

What Is Special About Christianity?

For God so loved the world that he gave his only begotten Son, that whosoever believes in him should not perish, but have everlasting life.

John 3:16

Be kind one to another, tenderhearted, forgiving one another, even as God for Christ's sake has forgiven you.

Ephesians 4:32

Perhaps as well as any two verses, these two encapsulate the meaning of Christianity. Being blessed and forgiven by God through Christ, we have the motivation to apply his teaching and example in our own lives. There is little here about the broad scope of society, a philosophical dissertation, or international war or peace. The emphasis is on each individual human being, precious in God's sight, alienated because of sin; the acknowledgment of our mistakes; and, through Christ who died for us, total forgiveness and reconciliation.

It is necessary to comprehend the uniqueness of Jesus as a human who was not famous or revered when he grew up in Nazareth. But when he began preaching and healing, the crowds flocked to him, and he gathered fervent followers—then and now—perhaps because of his words, his miracles, and his popularity. His ministry was universal but focused on individuals. His parables were about the value of one sheep lost out of one hundred, or one coin out of ten—the precious single soul.

When Jesus became famous, he was envied and despised by religious leaders who emphasized strict and sterile rules that tried to define the criteria for our acceptance by God. The personal aspect of God's love was secondary to them. Jesus, expected by many to be like the Pharisees, Sadducees, and scribes, shocked and often alienated his potential supporters by his revolutionary ideas. He cared for the outcasts and despised, the afflicted, the poor, or the different.

While negotiating a peace agreement at Camp David, I once shared a Friday night meal with Prime Minister Begin and other Israelis. I was impressed by their special prayers and ceremony, which lent a deeply religious quality to their Jewish meal, and as a result I could better understand the negative reaction when Jesus invited himself to supper with Zacchaeus, a sinful tax collector, and his friends. They were probably "birds of a feather" who drank too much, told ribald stories, and rarely if ever went to a synagogue to worship. When severely criticized, probably even by his own followers, Jesus replied, in effect, "I came to seek and to save the lost. The righteous don't need me" (Luke 19:10).

Jesus changed people's perspectives. A crippled man, obviously loved by his friends, was lowered through a hole in the roof into Jesus' presence. Just wanting him to be able to walk, his friends were as shocked as the Pharisees when Jesus said to him, "Your sins are forgiven." Sins were supposed to be forgiven only by God, after appropriate sacrifices were offered through the priests. When accused of blasphemy, Jesus added, almost as an afterthought, "Oh, by the way, take up your stretcher and carry it home." When the man did so, the people were amazed, filled with reverential fear, and they glorified God.

The primary emphasis of Jesus' teaching was on a proper relationship with God, with the physical healing clearly resulting from faith—in this case among the man's friends. This is just one of the many lessons from this remarkable event: people can be healed because of the faith of someone else. Jesus raised Lazarus through the faith of Mary and Martha, and he healed the children of a centurion and a synagogue leader because their fathers believed.

Jesus was a leader and a teacher who taught in synagogues, in people's homes, on the streets, in the countryside, and from boats. He taught with his words, his actions, his suffering, his death, and his resurrection. Through him we are given the assurance of God's forgiveness toward those of us who acknowledge our sins because we believe in Christ. We are reconciled with God through Jesus' love.

The result, for Christians, is that we should emulate what our Savior epitomized: kindness, tenderheartedness, forgiveness—and humility. When we assume an attitude of superiority, we depart from Christ, and forget his intense and unwavering love for us as individuals.

Chapter Nineteen

A Theology Primer

Therefore, since we are justified by faith, we have peace with God through our Lord Jesus Christ, through whom we have obtained access to this grace in which we stand; and we boast in our hope of sharing the glory of God. And not only that, but we also boast in our sufferings, knowing that suffering produces endurance, and endurance produces character, and character produces hope, and hope does not disappoint us, because God's love has been poured into our hearts through the Holy Spirit that has been given to us.

. . . Rarely will anyone die for a righteous person—though perhaps for a good person someone might actually dare to die. But God proves his love for us in that while we still were sinners Christ died for us. . . . So that, just as sin exercised dominion in death, so grace might also exercise dominion through

> justification leading to eternal life through Jesus Christ our Lord. Where sin abounded, grace did much more abound: that as sin has reigned unto death, even so might grace reign through righteousness unto eternal life by Jesus Christ our Lord.
>
> ROMANS 5:1–5, 7–8, 20–21

Most of us are leery about the word *theology*, considering it a controversial and confusing subject best addressed by college professors and authors of thick and incomprehensible books. Simply speaking, "theology" means the study of the nature of God and religious truth. Perhaps all of us have intriguing questions to be answered: What is my relationship to the Creator? To Christ? To other humans? How do good works relate to faith in God? How can we have inner peace when we are often frustrated, fearful, discouraged, or in despair? Theology deals with these vital questions.

We could spend a lifetime in study, delving ever more deeply into the nuances of religious scriptures and how they might be interpreted and applied to human consciousness and actions. While we may not all want to become biblical scholars, no one can expect to understand deeper meanings of the Scriptures with just a cursory reading. It's always valuable to think more deeply, and to seek written and verbal explanations. In early June 1997, I had a wonderful discussion with Hans Küng, one of the great theologians of our time. Although I had found some of his writings quite difficult to understand, his words in conversation were clear and incisive. He outlined for me a "Universal Declaration of Human Responsibility." With his help, a group of national leaders will use this document to strengthen and supplement the Universal Declaration of Human Rights that was adopted by the United Nations in 1948, following the Second World War.

The most famous and respected Christian theologian, Paul of Tarsus, wrote the passage at the beginning of this lesson in a letter to one of the new and struggling churches after the death and resurrection of Jesus. In this brief passage, he covers most of the basic elements of the Christian faith but uses some words whose meanings we need to explore somewhat carefully.

Let's look first at the word *hope.* Its modern meaning is to wish with some expectation of fulfillment. I might hope that I will live to be a hundred years old, that my grandchildren will always make good grades in school, that Navy's football team will beat Army's next year, or that it won't rain the next time I go fishing. In both 1976 and 1980, I hoped to win the presidential election. The archaic definition of the word was much closer to Paul's meaning: "to have confidence; to trust." In the letter to the Romans, there is absolutely no doubt that hope will be fulfilled; it's almost the same as "assurance."

"Justified" means that we are brought into a proper relationship with God, even though we have not merited this blessing because of our own character or good works. This seeming miracle is made possible by our faith, or trusting commitment to Christ and to God. Without this faith, we cannot be reconciled with God. The peace to which Paul refers is a transcendent sense of well-being and fulfillment, brought about by being in the presence of the Holy Spirit, as promised by Jesus.

Paul intends for human "righteousness" to mean absolute faith in and commitment to God. It has the connotation of fulfilling a promise or a covenant. God grants undeserved salvation to us sinners by his love, through Jesus Christ. This act is grace—a word that has the connotation of a free gift of joy, peace, and pleasure. Paul says in another letter, "By grace are you saved through faith; and that not of yourselves: it is the gift of God; not of works, lest any man should boast" (Ephesians 2:8–9).

There are two other interesting points that Paul makes in these few verses. One describes the unique sacrifice of Christ for us sinners—far beyond anything normally to be expected even for righteous people. The other, also surprising, is that we should welcome suffering because it leads us to endurance, then to character, and hope—hope that will never disappoint us.

With some understanding of justification, peace, faith, grace, righteousness, and hope, isn't this a wonderful message? Although many volumes have been written to analyze and explain Christian doctrine, the simple theology of this passage is all we need to know to understand the richness of our faith. Read it again, thoughtfully.

CHAPTER TWENTY

Joy in the Desert

It is written in Isaiah the prophet:
"I will send my messenger ahead of you,
who will prepare your way, a voice of one calling in the desert,
'Prepare the way for the Lord,
make straight paths for him.' "

And so John came, baptizing in the desert region and preaching a baptism of repentance for the forgiveness of sins.

MARK 1:2–4

The wilderness has always had a kind of mystique about it. Moses and the people of Israel wandered in the wilderness for forty years, and some of their most profound religious experiences took place there. We think of the miraculous manna from heaven and the water from the rock, both sent to sustain the Israelites in need, and the giving to Moses of the Ten Commandments while the people of Israel were camped in the desert beneath Mount Sinai. President Anwar Sadat urged Rosalynn and me to visit this site, and we enjoyed climbing the rocky slope of the mountain and talking to the priests who serve in the isolated monastery; we were amused when they showed us a flowering shrub that they called the "burning bush." Elijah and others of the prophets came out of the wilderness, and in later times Christian mystics, hermits, monks, and saints all retreated to the desert to be alone with God.

So the appearance of John the Baptist in the wilderness with his message of baptism and repentance was a natural part of the tradition of desert encounters with the Lord. The three key words in this passage from Mark are *baptism*, *repentance*, and *forgiveness*. Let's consider all three words and the relationship among them, which John was the first to describe.

Baptism is a ritual most Christian churches employ. In some churches, infants are baptized as a symbol of being part of the family of God. Usually, the baby is sprinkled with just a few drops of water on the head, symbolically cleansing the infant of sin. In other denominations, including my own Southern Baptist church, young people are baptized by full immersion in water, but only when they've reached an age where they can independently choose to dedicate themselves to Christ and become full members of the church. I was baptized at the age of eleven after having publicly accepted Christ as Savior during our church's annual revival.

Baptism is a joyous occasion and a meaningful ritual, but

for us Baptists—and I believe for most Christians—it is not necessary for salvation. Rather, it is a symbolic gesture that follows repentance and makes our inner commitment outwardly visible, demonstrating to our family, friends, and other church members our beginning a new life in Christ, as well as implanting that decision more firmly in our own memories, minds, and hearts. Jesus believed in the symbolic value of baptism and went himself to John to be baptized. Most Christians today follow his example. But we should remember that in all his teachings, Jesus emphasized the preeminence of inner truths over outward symbols. We are not saved by fasting, by offering sacrifices, by wearing sackcloth, by baptism, or even by good deeds. Faith, repentance, and the forgiveness of our sins through Christ are what saves us.

What is repentance, then, that precedes baptism and gives it meaning? It begins with self-analysis—an honest examination of our hearts and minds and of our actions, both the major commitments we make and the small, daily acts that determine the character of our lives. If we're honest, none of us can emerge from such self-analysis unscathed. For the Jews of Jesus' time, the standard against which they would measure their thoughts and deeds was the Ten Commandments and the Jewish laws as taught since the time of Moses. For Christians today, the standard is the life and teachings of Jesus. By either standard, none of us is perfect.

It's the nature of human life that "all have sinned and come short of the glory of God" (Romans 3:23). We may break one of God's laws by shading or twisting the truth, by hurting other people, by being insensitive to their needs, or by treating God's name with contempt. Or, more subtly, without apparently violating the law, we may fail to center our lives on the values that Jesus and the prophets taught. Rather than focus our time and energy on living the virtues of justice, compassion, truth, and giving to others, we let our lives become complacent and self-satisfied. This, too, is a failing that calls for repentance.

Repentance describes the inner action of recognizing our own failures and making the decision to change—to commit ourselves to a new course of action and a new way of life, more closely attuned to the model provided by Jesus Christ. This may require giving up some of our favorite habits, which makes it difficult and uncomfortable to do.

Fortunately, the message of John does not stop with baptism and repentance. It isn't complete without the third, most joyous element, forgiveness. And in the teachings of Jesus, and in his life, death, and resurrection, the principle of forgiveness comes to complete fruition. It is important not to wallow in guilt or embarrassment but to wipe the slate clean, turn away from the past, and fully accept the good news of Christ's complete and total forgiveness. We couldn't confess without the assurance of forgiveness. If self-examination brings us the sorrow and shame of recognizing our sinfulness, then accepting God's mercy, promised to us by Christ, makes possible a new life of peace, joy, and adventure. No longer uneasy about our past failings, we can concentrate today and tomorrow on a closer walk with God and our fellow human beings.

When we wander from God's ways, repentance is a necessary step. From time to time, we all need to visit the wilderness—if not a literal wilderness, then the spiritual desert of sorrow and regret that honest self-examination brings. But we aren't meant to live out our lives in solitude. We're meant to do as Jesus did: return from the wilderness to rejoin our brothers and sisters in the world, rejoicing in the good news of God's forgiveness and enjoying the new life of freedom, creativity, and love that it makes possible.

CHAPTER TWENTY-ONE

Are the Ten Commandments Enough?

And Cain talked with Abel his brother: and it came to pass, when they were in the field, that Cain rose up against Abel his brother, and slew him.

And the Lord said unto Cain, "Where is Abel your brother?" And he said, "I know not: Am I my brother's keeper?"

GENESIS 4:8–9

Breach for breach, eye for eye, tooth for tooth: as he has caused a blemish in a man, so shall it be done to him again.

LEVITICUS 24:20

> You have heard that it was said to the people long ago, "Do not murder, and anyone who murders will be subject to judgment." But I tell you that anyone who is angry with his brother will be subject to judgment. Again, anyone who says to his brother, "Raca," is answerable to the council. But anyone who says, "You fool!" will be in danger of the fire of hell.
>
> MATTHEW 5:21–22

The verses about the biblical command "Thou shall not kill" illustrate the revolutionary nature of Jesus Christ's teaching. Of course, the Old Testament commands were familiar to any Jew. But in his sermon, Jesus dramatically redefines its meaning. After all, most of us can say, "I haven't killed anyone; therefore, I haven't broken this commandment, and I must be okay with God." Right? "Wrong!" Jesus says. If we have anger in our hearts toward someone, or if we use words to assault or condemn another, we are as guilty as if we'd taken a person's life.

To me, this reinterpretation of God's law offers a disturbing challenge. I almost wish it were possible to wipe away the Sermon on the Mount and return to the original Ten Commandments—they are hard enough to live by! Yet as a follower of Jesus, I know this isn't an option, so it's important to understand what he is saying here.

The truth is that we're all familiar with the destructive power of words. We experience it in families, when an angry, judgmental father criticizes his children so harshly that he shatters their self-esteem; we see it when kids taunt an unpopular classmate in school, or when motorists threaten and curse each other in traffic jams.

I've certainly witnessed the potential violence in words during my political career. There are still white people in the South who can't say "Negro," "Black," or "African-American," and seem to strain when they use the word "Colored," preferring a more vicious word. And we all know the damaging, even lethal effect of anti-Semitic slurs. There are many other kinds of racial slurs. For example, when I was negotiating peace agreements in the Middle East, some Israeli leaders habitually referred to all Palestinians as "terrorists," drawing no distinctions among them. Rosalynn and I have visited the West Bank and Gaza many times, and we've met with people there from many walks of life: orange growers, pharmacists, schoolteachers, lawyers, housewives, fishermen, and so on. Contrary to what many people assume, a good number are Christians. All of them are Palestinians, and only a tiny portion would commit acts of terrorism. To use derogatory words to describe, and dismiss, a whole people is a destructive, dehumanizing act—as it is to employ anti-Semitic slurs or racist language of any kind.

Furthermore, in a troubled setting like the Middle East—or in Northern Ireland, the war-torn Balkan states, or many other places—violent language can and does feed physical violence. We must hate people to justify killing them, as explained in one of my poems.

WITH WORDS WE LEARN TO HATE

We take lives in times of peace
for crimes we won't forgive,
claiming some have forfeited
the right to live.

We justify our nation's wars
each time with words to prove we kill
in a moral cause.
We've cursed the names of those we fought:
the "Japs" instead of Japanese,
German Nazis or the "Huns,"
and "Wops" when they were enemies.

Later, they became our friends,
but habits live in memories.
So now, when others disagree
we hate again, and with our might,
war by war, name by dirty name,
prove we're right.

In the end, there is no way to draw a firm distinction between words and deeds. So when Jesus tells us that hatred spewed out in verbal form is akin to murder, he isn't exaggerating; he is expressing a fundamental truth, though one we'd prefer to overlook.

Jesus' words are still revolutionary today because they challenge our human tendency to build our lives in an egocentric, self-satisfied way. The things I do, the decisions I make, are usually chosen to meet my own needs and to promote my own self-image. And when I examine myself, I'm usually pretty pleased with what I see. I do the best I can, I say to myself; I'm not perfect, but I'm better than a lot of folks I know. I don't violate the law, and I certainly try to follow the Ten Commandments. All in all, I think I measure up to the standards of the other members of my church.

But Christ challenges this complacent self-image. He

demands more of us. We can't just fulfill the letter of God's commandments (difficult though that is to do at times); we must also fulfill its spirit, in our words and thoughts as well as our deeds.

It's not only a revolutionary message but an expansive one. If we want to follow Christ, the Sermon on the Mount tells us how: it requires us to enlarge our understanding of words such as *forgiveness*, *honesty*, *justice*, *compassion*, and *love*. Is it easy to do? No! But it's the avenue—the only avenue—to personal peace and peace in our world.

Chapter Twenty-Two

The New Message of Jesus

> Think not that I am come to destroy the law, or the prophets: I am come not to destroy, but to fulfill. For verily I say unto you, Till heaven and earth pass, one jot or one tittle shall in no wise pass from the law, till all be fulfilled.
>
> Matthew 5:17–18

Jesus brought such a revolutionary message that he was looked upon as a radical or, by some religious leaders, an anarchist. In the Sermon on the Mount, he reassured his listeners with the well-known words just quoted.

Still, there are striking differences between the general concepts of the Old Testament and the New Testament, relating to the character of God, the results of violation of or compliance with God's precepts, the identity of God's "chosen" people, and other issues of theological importance. Despite many efforts at reconciliation down through history, there are still sharp debates and even animosities created between some Christians and some Jews as we interpret the Scriptures.

One fact must be emphasized: It is a crime for any Christian to blame the Jewish people for the trial and crucifixion of Jesus. There is an inclination for some to forget that Jesus, Peter, Paul, and most of the earliest Christians were Jews, who shared their history, language, customs, and religious practices and faith with the Pharisees and Sadducees. Despite this, there was a continuing dispute between Jesus and many religious leaders of his day.

It is natural that, as in the time of the early church, there continues to be some disharmony today among Jews who await the coming of the Messiah and Christians who have faith that Jesus was and is the Messiah. In 1995, for instance, there were a series of confrontations in New York City between conservative rabbis and some Jews who had recently immigrated to the United States from Russia and had accepted Christ as Savior.

A major basis for contention is the interpretation of verses from the Book of Isaiah. Are the prophet's references to Jesus as the future Messiah, to the nation of Israel, to the contemporary Persian King Cyrus, or to some other leader? We can't resolve this argument, and there is no need for us to explore the differences in a judgmental way. But it is helpful for Christians to understand how our interpretations are different from those of non-Christians.

Let me take a few verses from Isaiah 49 as an example. We

Christians believe the prophet is referring to Jesus when he writes, "The Lord called me before I was born; while I was in my mother's womb He named me" (verse 1). And "It is too small a thing that you should be my servant to raise up the tribes of Jacob and to restore the preserved ones of Israel; I will also make you a light of the nations so that my salvation may reach to the end of the earth" (verse 6). Isaiah goes on to describe the Messiah as a suffering servant, and he and other prophets make it plain—at least to me—that the references are to Jesus. We know that Jesus himself declared that he was fulfilling the specific purpose that is described in the first two verses of Isaiah 61 (see chapter 2).

Jesus amazed his listeners with his interpretations of the Scriptures. In earlier times, "An eye for an eye and a tooth for a tooth" had been an enlightened commandment, limiting retribution for crime to an equal punishment; Jesus builds upon it by telling us to love our enemies, and to turn the other cheek if we are struck. "Thou shall not kill" is expanded to an admonition against hatred or cursing another person. Instead of animal sacrifices as a prerequisite for forgiveness, Jesus offered himself as the propitiation for our sins, and assured us of God's mercy and eagerness to forgive us as though we had not sinned at all.

Instead of a requirement that obeying laws or even doing good works serve as conditions for holiness, faith in God through Christ is sufficient for salvation. (It is interesting to note that, in the King James text, the word *faith* is used 245 times in the New Testament and only twice in the Old Testament.) Repeatedly, Jesus and his disciples violated the strict rules concerning the Sabbath, and he made the disturbing statement, "The Sabbath was made for man, and not man for the Sabbath" (Mark 2:27). He condemned convenient interpretation of the Scriptures to accommodate selfish goals concerning the condoning of divorce and caring for parents. Jesus reminded the religious leaders, "Moses said, 'Honor your father and your mother,' . . . but you say that if anyone tells father or mother, 'Whatever support you might have had from me is an offering to God,' then you no longer have to do anything for a father or mother, thus making void the word of God" (Mark 7:10–13).

One of the most significant and most condemned innovations of Christ—predicted by Isaiah—was his extension of salvation to the Gentiles. In his own ministry and his final command to the disciples, this was laid down as the foundation for the Christian church.

So there were a lot of differences in the prevailing interpretations of the Hebrew Scriptures and the Gospels, but Jesus assures us that there are absolutely no incompatibilities. Our Christian faith is best encapsulated in a few words he spoke to Nicodemus, an influential Pharisee and a ruler of the Jews: "For God so loved the world that He gave His only begotten son, that whosoever believes in him should not perish, but have eternal life. For God sent not His son into the world to judge the world, but that the world through him might be saved" (John 3:16–17).

With these words, we can understand not only the compatibility between the Old and New Testaments but also the transformations in our understanding of God and our personal relationship with our Creator that occurred with the coming of Jesus as the Messiah.

CHAPTER TWENTY-THREE

Christianity's Open Door

And certain men who came down from Judea taught the brethren, and said, "Unless you are circumcised after the manner of Moses, you cannot be saved." Therefore Paul and Barnabas had no small disagreement and argument with them . . . and determined to go to Jerusalem to the apostles and elders about this question. . . .

And when there had been much disputing, Peter rose up and said unto them, . . . "Now therefore why tempt God, to put a yoke upon the neck of the disciples, which neither our fathers nor we were able to bear? But we believe that through the grace of the Lord Jesus Christ we shall be saved, even as they."

ACTS 15:1–2, 7, 10–11

Shortly before I taught a Sunday School lesson based on this Bible passage in the summer of 1979, Rosalynn and I went to South Korea. We were overwhelmed by the dynamic Christian spirit that was sweeping the country. Five hundred thousand converts a year were joining churches, and a million people had assembled at the Seoul airport to hear Billy Graham preach. Our visit was the same year that the Moral Majority made the so-called Christian Right famous, and the moderate-conservative split came to a head in the Southern Baptist Convention. These were modern reminders of the kinds of successes and divisions that were seen in the early Christian church.

The inspired witnessing of Paul, Barnabas, Apollos, and other apostles was building churches in many Asian communities, including Antioch. The church members were sharing the message of Christ with remarkable results. There were also thousands of Christian Jews, who composed a strong church in Jerusalem (Acts 21:20).

The church in Antioch was on fire with evangelical fervor, reaching out to tell people about Christ, who had lived, died, and been resurrected as Savior. The primary message was that God's grace is all-encompassing, and that through faith in Jesus their sins could be forgiven and salvation was theirs. When someone came forward and said, "I believe in Jesus Christ as my savior, and want my sins to be forgiven," the leaders in Antioch said, "Welcome, brother!" or "Welcome, sister!" It was simple: A Christian was any person who was saved by the grace of God through faith in Jesus Christ.

It was a time of success and celebration, but differences were arising among believers that were serious enough to threaten the survival of the still infant church. Whether because of jealousy or honest theological beliefs, a group in the Jerusalem church delivered this divisive message to Antioch: "In order to become a Christian, you must first comply with all the Jewish customs as prescribed for our forefathers by Moses."

It is sometimes difficult for us to accept that God can be so generous as to accept and love us without reservation—there must be something else required. It seems natural that there should be some reasonable standards of previous conduct for a convert to Christianity. It was difficult for Jews in Jerusalem to forget about the ancient rules so clearly stated in Deuteronomy and Leviticus, and the dozens of other customs and practices that had formed the basis for their worship down through the centuries. Suppose a Roman soldier who had been persecuting the people of Israel came forward and said, "I have faith in Jesus Christ!" How could he be accepted as an equal among devout people?

We can understand both sides in this momentous debate. All of us, including me, tend to want to define what a Christian is. Unfortunately, it is only natural for us to make the definition of a "real" Christian fairly close to a description of our friends and ourselves. "After all," we think, "if we're not careful, we may just drift and be too inclusive. How could God have standards low enough to include sinners like that drunk lying on the sidewalk alongside a wine bottle, or that unwed mother who may still be sleeping around, or that jailbird who was found guilty of pushing drugs? Look at my friends and me. We're not addicts, our children were born in wedlock, and we've avoided a criminal life. Surely *we* represent what Christianity is all about."

This is exactly the attitude found among the Jewish Christians who condemned the open-door policy that Paul and other apostles had adopted. "At least let them adopt Jewish customs first" was the demand. It is interesting to me that James, leader of the Jerusalem church, chose Peter to enunciate the reply. We tend to exalt Paul as the preeminent theologian and founder of the early church, but at this time he was just an associate to the pastor Barnabas! It was Peter who had first received the Holy Spirit and later, with some reluctance, had introduced faith in Christ to Cornelius, a Gentile.

Now in our text, Peter speaks with perfect clarity about the choice between salvation through simple grace or salvation through circumcision plus adherence to intricate laws. This was a turning point in the life of the Christian church, one resolved through God's influence on Paul, Barnabas, Peter, James, and other leaders. In such an important and hotly debated issue, their unity was truly impressive.

I particularly like the last three words of Peter as he states the decision: "even as they." I like to interpret this by stretching it a little: "Isn't it great that God would let us big-shot Jerusalem Christians be saved just the way he let those Antioch Gentiles be saved!"

Paul and other Christians throughout the known world continued their evangelistic efforts based on the same nonexclusive requirement: "For whosoever shall call upon the name of the Lord shall be saved" (Romans 10:13). And "For by grace are you saved through faith; and that not of yourselves: it is the gift of God" (Ephesians 2:8).

When we face difficult decisions, we can learn from this episode what resources we have: God's guidance through prayer, sustained faith, and a willingness to turn to others who share that faith—minimizing the narrow and exclusive human demands and requirements we're tempted to impose.

CHAPTER TWENTY-FOUR

A House with Many Builders

Now I beseech you, brethren, by the name of our Lord Jesus Christ, that you all speak the same thing, and that there be no divisions among you; but that you be perfectly joined together in the same mind and in the same judgment. For I have been told that there are contentions among you. Now this I say, that every one of you says, 'I am of Paul'; 'and I of Apollos'; 'and I of Peter'; and 'I of Christ.' Is Christ divided? Was Paul crucified for you? Or were you baptized in the name of Paul?

1 CORINTHIANS 1:10–13

> Who then is Paul and who is Apollos? . . . I have laid the foundation, and another builds on it. But let everyone take heed how he builds on it. For there is only one foundation, which is Jesus Christ.
>
> 1 CORINTHIANS 3:5, 10–11

Paul had spent at least eighteen months among these people in Corinth, and he had been successful in establishing a strong congregation there. Now, sometime later, he was obviously concerned about divisions within the church, as members argued about conflicting loyalties to different preachers who had visited them. As usual, Paul went to the heart of the issue, emphasizing that there was only one foundation for their faith: Jesus Christ as the Son of God and the promised Messiah. He went on to say, "Don't you know that you are the temple of God?"

So Christ is the foundation, and we Christians are the edifices built on it. But how were these early Christians erecting the structure? Each group was beginning somewhere on the foundation and building in its own way. As the walls rose, they didn't match, and the roof was on sideways. Each group was pursuing its own ideas, and then they wound up blaming each other for the incompatibility.

What would Paul think about the modern Christian church? Is there a separate Methodist or Presbyterian or Mennonite foundation? Do Baptists have separate conservative and moderate foundations? Is there a Catholic or a Protestant foundation? Or should we all share the same foundation laid down by Jesus Christ? There are unpleasant, bitter divisions, and even wars, among those of us who compose the temple of God. Some want hardwood floors and others carpets; some like a hip roof and some prefer a more simple gable roof; there are strong preferences between wood and metal window frames; and how about the color of the front door? These are important issues, we insist, and we can't understand why anyone would disagree with us. Or perhaps it's best just to find a place on the foundation of Christ and build our own tiny houses out of straw or pasteboard, or plastic, and not even relate to others. After all, they are obviously wrong, and probably inferior!

We argue incessantly about separation of church and state, the priesthood of believers, ordination of women, prayer in schools, gay rights, predestination, inerrancy, public funds for church schools, and any number of other "crucial" issues. Perhaps worse than the Corinthians, we forget the solid, unquestionable, unifying foundation of our faith in the gentle Jesus, full of grace and truth. As Cecil Sherman, a leader of moderate Baptists, has said, "Too many churches are majoring in the minors."

We are given a foundation of excellence, truth, justice, service, sharing, and unselfish love. How should we build on this foundation? I can think of five ways, all admirable. One is good living, based on prayer and constant communication with God. A second is holiness, a life in which we are careful to avoid sin. A third is the spirit-filled, or charismatic life, exemplified by the disciples at Pentecost. Another is to be compassionate to the poor, perhaps building houses for them. And a final one is evangelism, telling people about Jesus Christ.

There is certainly nothing wrong with any of these. Do we need prayer, to be holy, to be filled with the Spirit, to minister to the needy, to witness for Christ? Certainly we do. The problem is when we Christians select one or two of these ways and say, "This is the religious foundation on which I build my life, and those who build in other ways are wrong." As Paul would advise, we need to meld them all into a beautiful and harmonious structure.

How can this be done? Harmony can be reached by referring to the most exalted goals of Christianity. It seems illogical, but these are the ones that require the most modest talents, intelligence, and influence. When we remember the pure teachings of Jesus, we realize that any human being can espouse truth, justice, humility, and compassion. This is where we find the common foundation for our Christian lives.

Christians in the World

CHAPTER TWENTY-FIVE

The Christian Citizen

> Submit yourselves for the Lord's sake to every authority instituted among men: whether to the king, as the supreme authority, or to governors, who are sent by him to punish those who do wrong and to commend those who do right. . . . Show proper respect to everyone: love the brotherhood of believers, fear God, honor the king.
>
> 1 PETER 2:13, 17

How startling this message of Peter's must have seemed in his day! Consider that he wrote these words when the emperor of Rome, the supreme political authority throughout most of the known world, was severely oppressing the Christian church, imprisoning and even killing the followers of

Jesus on account of their faith. For Peter to write a letter urging Christians to submit loyally to the government is, indeed, a curious act.

The same paradox has confronted Christians in many times and places. Revolution against British rulers gave birth to America. Germany under Hitler is another obvious example. Driven by a monstrous philosophy and supported by twisted distortions of Christian teaching, the Nazi regime carried out the greatest crime of modern history. How could Christians submit themselves for the Lord's sake to such an authority?

Occasionally, Rosalynn and I visit the African nation of Sudan, currently ruled by a fundamentalist Muslim government. Under their strict interpretation of Islamic law, known as Sharia, only Muslim men have full rights as citizens. Non-Muslim believers in God (other People of the Book, as they are sometimes called, including Christians and Jews) are second-class citizens; and nonbelievers are given few basic rights. What is the proper role of a Christian living under such a regime?

And there are examples closer to home. We all disagree with our own government at times. Fortunately, in a free society, there are peaceful ways to change the government with our choice of leaders. And between elections, we can use the power of our voices to influence laws and policies.

Nonetheless, even in a democracy there are times when submission to the government is not a sufficient response to injustice. When our sons were in college, movements for civil rights, the end of the Vietnam War, and environmental quality were examples of concerted public effort by millions of people, sometimes including acts that violated the law. It was the willingness of courageous protesters to break such laws and accept the punishment for breaking them that forced the nation to recognize the injustice of the laws and, ultimately, to change them.

Almost twenty years later, our daughter, Amy, was arrested four times, for demonstrating against apartheid in South Africa and against what she considered illegal activities of the CIA during the Contra war in Nicaragua. There was an extended trial on the latter charge, but she and her associates were declared innocent because the Massachusetts jury decided that their peaceful demonstration was a small crime intended to prevent a greater one.

Clearly, Peter is not saying that a particular government, with whatever laws and policies it currently enforces, is to be looked upon as sacred or unchangeable. If he'd believed that, he and his fellow Christians would not have faced prison and even death because they worshiped Christ and not the Roman gods.

By considering both Peter's teachings in this epistle and Paul's to the Romans (13:1–10), we can see their true meaning. In general, government is a necessary, often beneficent force, which preserves peace and order, punishes those who commit crimes against others, and to one degree or another gives citizens a voice in shaping the policies that affect their lives. To this extent, governments deserve our respect and support. As inhabitants of our world, Christians usually have a responsibility to play a positive role in supporting the social order for the good of all.

But when a government seeks to impose laws that are

unjust and contrary to God's commands, our responsibility changes. Under those circumstances, we should start by looking within ourselves: How do we understand God's will for us and for the world? What talents, abilities, and influence can we bring to bear on the situation? And in light of the answers to these questions, how can we work to moderate or modify government policies or, if necessary, dramatically change the government itself?

What each of us feels called upon to do as a Christian citizen may vary greatly. To vote our consciences, to express our beliefs in speaking and writing, to work on behalf of particular candidates or run for offices ourselves—all these are natural and important roles. In some circumstances, more dramatic steps may be needed, including forceful public protests or even civil disobedience. And sometimes the rejection of oppressive authority requires the willingness to accept punishment: prison, as in the case of Paul, or even death, as the life of Jesus illustrates.

To decide the right course of action in any given circumstances may not be easy. It requires thoughtful consideration, a spirit of openness, cooperation, and love, even toward those with whom we deeply disagree, and, of course, the seeking of God's guidance through prayer. The weak and oppressed are the ones most likely to turn to Christ. The essence of his teaching is to enhance justice, truth, freedom, service, and love. This must be our guiding light when we are considering how best to fulfill our role as Christians in society.

CHAPTER TWENTY-SIX

Do We Really Believe in Human Rights?

And Ahab said to Naboth, "Give me your vineyard, for a herb garden near my house. And I will give you a better vineyard, or, if you prefer, I will give you a fair price for it." But Naboth said to Ahab, "The Lord forbids that I sell my father's inheritance to you." And Ahab went into his house sad and displeased, and lay down upon his bed, and turned away his face, and would not eat. . . . And his wife Jezebel said, "I will give you the vineyard."

. . . And she put Naboth on a pedestal, and got two men to witness against him. And they carried him out and stoned him to death. . . . And Ahab got up and went to Naboth's vineyard, to take possession of it.

1 KINGS 21:2–4, 7, 12–13, 16

On April 25, 1979, Georgi Vins was in a cattle car in Siberia, being transported as an exile in his own country. Four days later, he was in a Sunday School class I was teaching at First Baptist Church in Washington. Perhaps not coincidentally, the title of the lesson was "A Cry for Justice."

As president, I had agreed with President Leonid Brezhnev to trade two convicted Soviet spies for the release of five men whom I considered human rights heroes, along with their families. Georgi Vins was a Baptist pastor who had been sent to Siberia because he insisted on professing his Christian faith despite orders from the Communist dictators to remain silent. He had no idea where he was being taken until he and the four others were placed on a commercial jet, destined for the United States. When he left Russia his head was shaven, he had a Bible in his hand, and I was told later that my photograph was hidden in his shoe.

A few days later, on Law Day, I spoke before the chief justice of the Supreme Court, the attorney general, and other leaders and referred to this lesson. Let me quote a few sentences from this speech:

> The highest goal that a government or societal structure can hope to achieve is justice. It's an end in itself; it's a means to an end; and it's a pursuit that is never completely realized. There are always challenges to it brought about by the fallibilities of human beings, the intense pressure of competition in a free society, the constraint of liberty where freedom does not exist. It's a responsibility on us, as it is on the leaders of every nation on earth.

The deprivation of justice is a serious matter. Those of us who don't suffer much from it can observe it, if we are sensitive. Quite often we benefit from an injustice, because those with power, wealth, or social prominence are very likely to profit when an advantage is meted out to our peers who, in gaining some advantages for themselves, cause those same benefits to accrue to us.

And if we stand silent and reap the benefits of injustice, then we ourselves are equally culpable with those who initiated the injustice.

The case of Ahab, Jezebel, and Naboth provides a good example of these premises. Ahab was a rich and powerful king who ruled Israel from 874 to 853 B.C. He professed to honor the laws of God and his nation, but he also worshiped idols and violated the basic principles of justice. He had married Jezebel, a Phoenician princess, who was worse than her husband and an evil influence on him.

In refusing to give up his small garden plot, Naboth was complying with Hebrew law expressed in Leviticus against the sale of land and also honoring the memory of his ancestors. Ahab's lying in bed, pouting, and refusing to eat was a strange reaction for a monarch, and we don't really know how much of it was designed to bring about the subsequent actions of Jezebel. But there is never any indication that Ahab questioned what she did.

There were religious laws in Israel designed to ensure justice and protect human rights. A king could not forcefully take property from any citizen, and no one could be convicted of a crime without two witnesses agreeing on evidence. Jezebel exalted Naboth to arouse public jealousy against him, bribed two false witnesses to swear he had blasphemed God and the king, and had him executed. Her fellow conspirators and many other citizens knew what she was doing, but they all looked the other way because they were rewarded, feared the king or wanted to ingratiate themselves with him, were jealous of Naboth, or just didn't want to be involved.

The lesson for us is that injustice can be perpetrated in a society only with the complicity or acquiescence of others who benefit or avoid responsibility while denying knowledge. As Christians, do we have a responsibility for those in our own communities or in other nations who are suffering, from either deprivation or persecution? Four well-known questions help to give us the answer. One was when God searched for Adam in the Garden of Eden: "Where are you?" Another was to Cain: "Where is your brother?" And the response: "Am I my brother's keeper?" One more was to Jesus: "Who is my neighbor?"

I wrote a poem a few years ago about this theme:

HOLLOW EYES, BELLIES, HEARTS

We chosen people, rich and blessed,
rarely come to ask ourselves
if we should share our voice or power,
or a portion of our wealth.

We deal with problems of our own,
and claim we have no prejudice
against the people, different, strange,
whose images we would dismiss:

Hollow eyes in tiny faces,
hollow bellies, gaunt limbs, there
so far away. Why grieve here
for such vague, remote despair?

Human debris tries to reach
a friendly port, however far.
We can't pay them mind forever,
wretched dregs from an ugly war.

With apartheid's constant shame
Black miners slave for gems and gold.
The wealth and freedom are not theirs;
White masters always keep control.

Bulldozed houses, olive trees axed;
terrorist bombs, funeral wails;
no courts or trials, prison still.
The land is holy, hate prevails.

One alone in a Chinese square
confronted tanks, while others fled.
He stood for freedom for us all,
but few care now if he's jailed or dead.

Visits in the dark of night
by lawful thugs—indrawn breaths
of fear, and then the last farewells.
The death squads won't admit the deaths.

Torture, murder . . . bitter loss
of liberty and life. But they
are friendly tyrants! What would all
our cautious questioning convey?

Why think of slaves, nameless deaths?
Best be still, as in other days.
Response was bland to Hitler's deeds.
Should we condemn our fathers' ways?

We chosen few are truly blessed.
It's clear God does not want us pained
by those who suffer far away.
Are we to doubt what He ordained?

If I am my brother's keeper, it's not enough for me to learn about or even pray about his troubles. I'm called upon to act on his behalf, even when that requires fighting injustice and tyranny.

CHAPTER TWENTY-SEVEN

Woman and Man, Equal Before God

Wives, be submissive to your husbands so that, if any of them do not believe the word, they may be won over without talk by the behavior of their wives, when they see the purity and reverence of your lives. . . . Husbands, in the same way be considerate as you live with your wives, and treat them with respect as the weaker partner and as heirs with you of the gracious gift of life, so that nothing will hinder your prayers.

1 PETER 3:1–2, 7

There are passages in the Bible that are very difficult for people today to accept, and this is certainly an example. To one degree or another, almost all of us believe in the liberation of women and the equality of the sexes, and this makes Peter's words "be submissive" quite troubling to us. Paul makes a few comments that are very similar, and some religious leaders distort these verses to discriminate against women. This creates enough of a problem so that some Christians, including our daughter, Amy, have withdrawn from the church. And those of us who remain loyal churchgoers are nonetheless made uneasy by the misinterpretation of these verses.

How do we deal with this uneasiness? It's tempting to try to ignore these troublesome biblical passages, saying, "Oh, that was written 2,000 years ago—it doesn't apply to me now." But that's a dangerous path to take. We need to believe—and as Christians, most of us do believe—that the total wisdom of the Bible does apply to us today. If we begin eliminating verses that we consider outdated, we may find ourselves choosing just those verses that happen to suit our own temperaments, habits, or foibles. The Bible should help correct our personal tastes, not just reinforce them.

At the same time, it's true that the Bible, though inspired by God, was written by fallible human beings who shared the knowledge and beliefs of their times. The science and astronomy of the Bible are inaccurate by modern standards (speaking of the earth's "four corners," for example), and biblical writers in New Testament times still wrote as if slavery were a legitimate social institution that should not be questioned. So it is appropriate to consider the times in which the Bible was written when interpreting the meaning of Scripture and its message for us today.

In the Mediterranean world of the first century, when Jesus, Peter, and Paul all lived, women were forbidden to play any leading role in society. A single woman was the property of her father, and a married woman was the property of her husband. Women did not speak for themselves in the houses of worship, in the public squares, or in other forums. Both literally and figuratively, the woman walked several paces behind her husband.

As we see in the Gospels, Jesus challenged this prevailing suppression of women. Many of his most faithful and prominent followers were women, and throughout Jesus' travels he lived and spoke with women in terms of virtual equality. After his death, women were the first witnesses of the resurrection, and they were the ones who proclaimed the good news of his rising.

If we examine this lesson's text objectively, we see a strong element of equality, perhaps very startling to early Christians and nonbelievers. Also, Paul, who made some comments about women's not speaking in religious services, directly contravened this concept in the sixteenth chapter of Romans. He lists twenty-seven people who played a prominent role in the early church; ten of them were women. Phoebe was a minister or deacon, Junia was "outstanding among the apostles," and Priscilla was a pastor who worked with Paul and corrected the beliefs of Apollos, a great preacher.

To me, all of this is clear evidence that Christ intended women to play a major—even equal—role in his church. An increasing number of Christians believe, as I do, that no position, including deacon, pastor, or priest, should be withheld from women. Shortly after I left the White House, I served on a committee to draft a new constitution for our church. I proposed that both men and women should be permitted to serve as deacons. At the time, the proposal received only four votes at the church conference, but more recently our members voted to authorize women deacons.

One of the most pertinent verses of Scripture comes from Paul's letter to the Galatians, when he reminds them, "For as many of you as have been baptized into Christ have put on Christ. There is neither Jew nor Greek, there is neither bond nor free, there is neither male nor female: for ye are all one in Christ Jesus" (3:27–28).

An overall premise is that all of us, as equals, should accept the social order of the time and place where God has placed us and do our best to live loyally and faithfully as Christians, while questioning or challenging societal norms when they violate the equality of God's love and grace.

CHAPTER TWENTY-EIGHT

Leadership and Reformation

Then, at the evening sacrifice, I rose from my self-abasement, with my tunic and cloak torn, and fell on my knees with my hands spread out to the Lord my God and prayed: "O my God, I am too ashamed and disgraced to lift up my face to you, because our sins are higher than our heads and our guilt has reached to the heavens. . . . But now, for a brief moment, the Lord our God has been gracious in leaving us a remnant and giving us a firm place in his sanctuary, and so our God gives light to our eyes and a little relief in our bondage."

EZRA 9:5–6, 8

Ezra played an important part in the history of the Israelites during the time of the Babylonian captivity some 2,500 years ago, when the Jewish people were ruled by the Persian Empire. Born and raised in a Jewish community in Babylon, Ezra was among the Jews who returned to Jerusalem under the decree of King Cyrus with a mandate to rebuild the Temple, their traditional center of worship. And Ezra, a scholar and teacher of the Law, brought with him to Jerusalem his own copy of the Hebrew Scriptures, which became the basis for a revival and renewal of the faith. So important was Ezra's role that some scholars call him the father of Judaism.

When Ezra returned to the Holy City, he was appalled to observe the fragmented state of the Hebrew faith. He decided that much of the problem had been caused by intermarriage between the Jews and the neighboring tribes. Marriage between people of different races and ethnic backgrounds is a natural thing; it will happen whenever groups live closely together. And during the period when the Jews were in Babylon, they had continued to worship their own God, even in the midst of pagan worship and beliefs. In many ways they had become part of Babylonian society; many had become landowners, some had grown wealthy. In this relatively comfortable situation, it's understandable that some of the Jews would have married people from among the neighboring tribes.

But for Ezra, this was a serious mistake and a sin. The ancient law arose from a concern that, if the Jews married pagan men and women, the Jewish faith would inevitably be diluted and weakened. Ezra was called by God to speak out against this danger, and he does so in the ninth chapter of the book that bears his name.

Notice some significant things about how Ezra conveys this message that may be helpful to us. First, he begins by speaking openly to God about their sins. When we have gone astray in our lives, the first, essential step in returning to the right path is confession, difficult and painful though it may be. Second, look at the words Ezra uses to describe the Israelites' misdeeds: *our* sins, *our* guilt. Ezra had not married a Canaanite woman or strayed from the prescribed teachings and worship of God, but as the spiritual leader of the Jews, he felt and spoke as if he were equally guilty. Ezra didn't fall into the trap many of us do today, distancing himself from the wrongdoing of others, as if proud of his superiority. It's easy to fool ourselves this way. Sin is a common human condition. Ezra didn't preach down to his fellow Jews. Rather, he said, "I am in the same boat, morally and spiritually, with all of our people, and we pledge ourselves to do something about it together."

Based on this attitude of realism and humility, and on his willingness to confess sins and ask God for forgiveness, Ezra was able to lead a religious reformation that helped saved Judaism. The Israelites rededicated themselves to teaching and practicing their traditional faith, and vowed to marry among themselves.

What does the word *reformation* imply? Literally, to re-form, to change in a way that is dramatic and total, closer to revolution than to evolution. When a pine tree grows to maturity, that is a gradual change. But if we chop down a tree and burn it, or cut boards from the wood and use them to build a house, that is a reformation. For a number of years, my brother, Billy, was a hopeless alcoholic, often embarrassing to his friends and alienated from his family. But with the unwavering love and support of his wife, Sybil, he overcame this affliction and spent the last decade of his life without alcohol. In fact, after this reformation Billy and Sybil became national leaders in ministering to other alcoholics, many of whom said, "If Billy can do it, so can I."

Reformation is an essential aspect of life. But I know from personal experience that moral and spiritual reformation of a society or of one human heart is not easy to bring about. It often takes both a crisis and the inspiration of another person, like Ezra or Sybil, to show a society or an individual the need for change and the path that must be followed to achieve it.

Ezra had several qualities that made him an effective voice for reformation. The Israelites felt that he was one of them, sharing their weaknesses and their sin and striving with them to repent, atone, and begin anew. And he was a man of prayer, opening his heart and speaking freely and honestly to God about the rights and wrongs of his people. In return, he understood the will of God and had the ability and strength to lead the Israelites. At the same time, Ezra knew that true power arises from the guidance of God, not from human talents or pride.

What are the areas of life in which today's society is desperately in need of reformation? We accept now without question the violation of God's laws. Reaction to the recent discharge from the Air Force of a female bomber pilot showed that the general public is inclined to criticize the military for enforcing rules that forbid adultery, lying, or disobeying orders. It's easy to think of other examples of the need for reform: society's acceptance of the plight of the hungry and the homeless, the suffering of innocents in needless wars, the gradual destruction of our natural environment, the evils of racial, ethnic, and religious hatred.

Fortunately, God's power to bring about dramatic change

in the human heart, beginning with confession and repentance, is available to us today just as it was to the Israelites in the days of Ezra. As Christians, all of us are capable of and trained for leadership. We can help at least one other person. All that's missing is our willingness to pray, to obey, and to act as he did.

CHAPTER TWENTY-NINE

What Can One Person Do?

> And Jesus came and spoke to his disciples, saying, "All power is given unto me in heaven and in earth. Go therefore, and teach all nations, baptizing them in the name of the Father and of the Son, and of the Holy Ghost: Teaching them to observe all things whatsoever I have commanded you; and lo, I am with you always, even unto the end of the world."
>
> MATTHEW 28:18–20

In 1976, two unprecedented things happened in the small congregation of the Baptist Church in the village of Plains, Georgia. One family was chosen to go to the White House, and another family was assigned to be missionaries in West Africa. One has become famous, but the other is, justifiably, more honored in our church. For as long as I can remember, our most exalted heroes have been missionaries who go to foreign lands to serve Christ.

Jerome Ethridge was an agronomist at the Southwest Georgia Experiment Station, located about a mile east of Plains. He was not a preacher, knew no foreign language, and had no religious education except as a member and deacon in our church. He and his wife, Joann, were given rudimentary training as missionary recruits, sent to France to learn the language, and then assigned to Sokodé, Togo. They ran a Christian library and taught languages to the young people who came by for books. Hundreds learned to read and write, but there was little chance for Jerome to use his agricultural skills or to be an effective witness for Christ.

When the opportunity arose, they were able to go to a much smaller and more isolated village named Moretan, in East Mono, a region of Togo. There, among people who mostly worshiped nature or crafted idols, the Ethridges assessed how they might meet urgent human needs. The greatest need was for drinking water, which was plentiful only during the rainy season. At other times, the women had to walk as far as sixteen miles each day to get water. With diesel well-drilling equipment furnished by some North Carolina Baptists and the help of local villagers, Jerome drilled 167 wells, 130 of them successful and capped with hand pumps. Over a period of eight years, every village within eighty miles of Moretan received a working well.

Next, with a leased bulldozer, Jerome constructed twenty-one deep ponds that hold the seasonal rainwater throughout the year. He stocked the ponds with tilapia, a fast-growing fish that provides a much-needed source of protein for the villagers. During these years, he also used his agronomy skills to help the people increase greatly their production of food crops, forage for livestock, and trees that provide wood for cooking and home construction. Joann works with families on health and education projects, helped build a pharmacy, and provides transportation to a distant hospital for those too ill to be treated locally.

Finally, Jerome was ready to undertake a long-postponed task, to correct a problem that had always afflicted all of East Mono. For four months of each year, rain changed the Mono River into an impassable barrier, isolating the area from the rest of Togo. Using cement furnished by his North Carolina friends, he and local volunteers built a bridge. When Rosalynn and I visited the Ethridges, we were amazed to see the 230-foot concrete span across the stream.

Much like Moses, Jerome Ethridge has modest skills as an orator, and he doesn't claim to be an expert on religious or theological subjects. He and his wife have just tried to serve the needy people around them, all without publicity or fanfare, and always in the name of Christ.

In addition to providing a better life for many people, what have the Ethridges accomplished in a religious sense? There are now 5,000 active members in eighty-one Christian congregations in East Mono, each served by a local pastor. This is vivid proof of what just two people can do, inspired by faith in Christ and willing, like their Savior, to be humble servants.

To Know and Worship

CHAPTER THIRTY

A Message in Creation

> That which is known about God is evident within them; for God made it evident to them. For since the creation of the world, His invisible attributes, His eternal power and divine nature have been clearly seen, being understood through what has been made, so that they are without excuse.
>
> ROMANS 1:19–20

My university degree is in engineering, and my postgraduate studies were in physics and nuclear technology. Since my college days, I have encountered a number of notable scientists, a few of them willing to discuss theological issues with me. My family and I spent one unforgettable evening with the late Carl Sagan, one of the most famous astronomers.

We drove from the White House to meet him at the vice president's home, where we enjoyed a slide lecture and then went over to the Naval Observatory, which is almost in the front yard. While everyone took turns looking through the large telescope, I asked Sagan about astronomical theories. He explained that either the universe is expanding indefinitely from a tiny point or "singularity" (the Big Bang theory) or, depending upon the amount of dark matter in the heavens, the entire world would expand further and then collapse on itself. He denied believing in a Supreme Being but didn't want to talk—at least to me—about what alternative might exist for the creation of it all.

St. Paul didn't know anything about cosmological theories, nebulae, or even telescopes, but he had a vivid concept of the grandeur of creation. He made it clear in the letter to the Romans that even if we have never read a Bible, listened to a sermon, or heard the name of Jesus, Moses, or Isaiah, we should still know God through the awareness of what has been created and the apparent miracles that surround us.

We resent the suffering, injustice, and violence in our society, and observe that the unrighteous often seem to prosper while the finest people we know seem to suffer unfairly. Even people who call themselves Christians may have occasional doubts about God, but we often feel that if we could only see miracles like those recorded in the Bible, then we would believe.

Paul responds to these kinds of doubts. He makes it clear that the rejection of our Creator despite all the clear evidence around us is foolish. What is that clear evidence? Do we have modern-day miracles on which to predicate our faith?

About 400 years before Paul wrote his letter, the Greek philosopher Aristotle had pronounced that everything had to be perfect, which implied for him that everything in the heavens had to be spherical and nothing new could ever be discovered about them. For centuries, religious leaders predicated their teaching of Paul's text on the centrality of the earth, with the sun, moon, and stars revolving around it. It was not until 1610 that Galileo used his new telescope to ascertain that the earth revolves around the sun, and announced that the Vatican should not base its religious tenets on scientific theories that would always be changing with increasing knowledge. He was condemned by philosophers and the church, and was excommunicated and imprisoned. (It's interesting to note that Pope John Paul II announced in 1992 that the Vatican had been wrong.)

This historic event illustrates that human interpretation of Bible texts cannot limit God's revelations through science about the universe. Evidence increases that a Supreme Being must have orchestrated the astounding things that we can now observe with improved instruments and shared knowledge. We know now that our sun is just one star of average size, that there are billions of stars in our Milky Way galaxy, and then billions of other galaxies. All of this is expanding at an enormous rate, as Carl Sagan explained to my family that night.

We've also learned incredible things about such wonders as the evolution of an infant in the womb and the complexity of the eye, and we now know that a human brain contains more connecting points than there are stars in the universe!

Some years ago a professor at Emory University, where I now lecture, declared, "God is dead!" Although his premises were widely misinterpreted, he was instantly famous, and theological debates raged. Many believers chortled over the response "God can't be dead. I talked to Him this morning." Innate faith and our own knowledge and experiences as Christians are adequate for most of us. But when we have doubts or feel our faith weaken, reassurance comes from the vastness, complexity, order, and beauty of God's creation.

CHAPTER THIRTY-ONE

The Mystery of Resurrection

> But someone may ask, How are the dead raised? With what kind of body will they come? How foolish! What we sow does not come to life unless it dies. When we sow, we do not plant the body that will be, but just a seed, perhaps of wheat or of something else. . . . So it will be with the resurrection of the dead.
>
> 1 CORINTHIANS 15:35–37, 42

How can we believe in life after death? How can we conceive of such mysteries? These have always been profound questions for most of the world's religions. This was the main issue that divided the Pharisees and Sadducees, who claimed that there was no life after death. In the early Christian church, doctrinal questions like these also led to bitter arguments and even permanent, hostile separations between church groups. In his first letter to the Corinthians, Paul addresses these questions in an effort to explain the mystery and to heal one such schism.

How does Paul explain life after death? He tries to focus our attention on the most basic, inarguable facts. Paul begins with a commonly recognized earthly truth, something familiar to everyone in a farming community: When we plant a seed, what later appears is completely different from the seed, totally transformed in its character. A stalk of corn or a peanut vine doesn't resemble the seed kernel that is planted.

The same is true of every living thing. Take a caterpillar. It makes a little cocoon that may look like a piece of dead leaf, out of which miraculously comes a lovely creature. There is nothing in the appearance of a homely, crawling caterpillar that would let us predict, "That's going to become a beautiful butterfly!" The transformation is mysterious, even seemingly miraculous.

Paul uses this kind of analogy to say that our present physical bodies may have little relationship to our appearance after the resurrection. His message is simple: Don't even try to guess what we may become after death and resurrection. To argue over such things is foolish.

Paul goes on to say, "The body that is sown is perishable, it is raised imperishable . . . it is sown a natural body, it is raised a spiritual body" (verses 42, 44). This is a beautiful yet still mysterious explanation. The concept of a heavenly life remains elusive. It's hard for us to envision things that we can't put directly into human terms. We fall back on childlike concepts of heaven: pearly gates, golden streets, angels with wings sitting on clouds. Though we know these images are inadequate and inaccurate, they may be the best we can do.

Mary Magdalene and the other women had met the resurrected Jesus and told the rest of the disciples about it. Peter and John had seen the empty tomb with their own eyes. And later, Jesus appeared to all the apostles, to two grieving followers on the road to Emmaus, and to as many as 500 others assembled together. Most of them, Paul said, were still alive at the time the biblical accounts were written. The last dramatic appearance of Christ was to Paul himself. The resurrection of Jesus Christ is a truth on which all Christians agree, and it's enough for us to face death—and a future life.

Fortunately, it's not important for us to understand the concept of heaven or the life of the resurrected body. As Paul reminds us, we don't need to know the details of what awaits us. What we need to know is that Christ died for us and lived again, and that, through faith in him, we, too, can enjoy a resurrected life—whatever it may be like.

Chapter Thirty-Two

Ready to Worship

Lord, who may dwell in your sanctuary?
Who may live on your holy hill?
He whose walk is blameless and who does what is righteous.

Psalm 15:1–2

This Psalm excerpt challenges us to consider how we can be worthy to enter the presence of God. The sanctuary and the holy hill both describe the Temple in Jerusalem, the center of worship in ancient Israel. The psalmist is asking, "How can we prepare ourselves to spend time with God in a holy place?"

When I was a child of four or five, the offering envelopes that we used in our Sunday School class had accomplishments with points listed on the back. We got 20 points for being at church, 20 points for being on time, 30 points for studying our lesson, 20 points for bringing our Bible, another 10 points for giving an offering in the envelope. Every week, we'd fill out the envelopes and hand them in with our scores marked. A few kids would earn all 100 points. If we got 100 four Sundays in a row, we'd get a special treat, like an extra cookie. We had a clear idea in those days what it meant to be worthy, at least in the eyes of our Sunday School teacher—and what the reward would be!

Many of us have gotten away from preparing ourselves for worship. Instead, we assess church services almost as if they were shows put on to entertain us. When someone asks us, "How was church today?" we might answer, "Well, the choir did their best, but they obviously need more practice." Or we might say, "The sermon was too long. The pastor went on until five minutes after twelve and could easily have been finished ten minutes sooner." But this is not the way to think about a worship service. When we speak like this, we're putting the responsibility for worship on other people. What makes a successful worship service is not the beauty of the music or the eloquence of the preacher or even the friendliness of the greeting we receive. Instead, it's the presence of God in our hearts, and that depends on our attitude and what we are seeking.

We need to be prepared, mentally and spiritually, to participate fully in worship. This is something to consider as we make our way to church on Sunday morning, or whenever we worship. We must ask ourselves, "What is the state of my mind and heart as I go to church or approach God in prayer?"

Am I worshiping in a spirit of pride and complacency, or with a searching and humble heart, ready to receive whatever good thing God has in store for me? Is my mind closed to new ideas and to a challenging or surprising message, or have I tried to acknowledge my shortcomings and am I searching for the presence of the Holy Spirit—even if it may disturb me? I confess that it is a challenge for me even to concentrate on what the words mean and not let my mind wander when I join in reciting the Lord's Prayer.

Perhaps when the psalmist says that we must be righteous to dwell in God's sanctuary, this is part of what he has in mind: that we should go to public worship not to be entertained but to seek new and exciting possibilities for our lives as children of God. And I doubt that the only sanctuary of God is inside a church or synagogue. No matter where we are, we can always find the presence of God.

CHAPTER THIRTY-THREE

Pray Without Ceasing

I have posted watchmen on your walls, O Jerusalem; they will never be silent day or night. You who call on the Lord, give yourselves no rest, and give him no rest till he establishes Jerusalem and makes her the praise of the earth.

ISAIAH 62:6–7

We all experience rejection. When I was a child, the big boys would choose up baseball teams at recess, and I would often be the last one chosen, because I was small and not a very good athlete. I would have given half my savings from selling boiled peanuts if they would have chosen me as one of the early ones! But being left out, abandoned, or rejected happens to all of us at times. This passage describes the prophet

Isaiah's sense that God has forsaken the people of Israel. (Many of the earlier chapters of the Book of Isaiah describe the sins of the Israelites, and the desolation, despair, and suffering they had undergone as a result.) Isaiah's response in this time of tribulation is, perhaps, surprising. He calls on sentinels—watchmen—to sit on the walls of Jerusalem, God's holy city, and offer incessant, constant, repetitive prayer, until the wishes of the Jewish people for reconciliation with God are granted. It reminds me of the apostle Paul's admonition to the early Christians, hundreds of years later: "Pray without ceasing" (1 Thessalonians 5:17).

The message to us is this: Never give up on God, who always answers our prayers. Sometimes the answer is "Wait" or "No," or perhaps, as our pastor, Dan Ariail, says, "You've got to be kidding!" Then we must reassess what we are seeking. Continuing to pray hopefully in the face of profound disappointment seems contrary to human nature. Why should we do it? Because invariably we can learn and grow in the process.

One of the most humorous stories of Jesus was about the woman who irritated an unjust judge so persistently, even at his home at night, that he finally made a proper ruling (Luke 18:1–7). In another story, immediately following the Lord's Prayer, Jesus told of a man who had an unexpected guest and went to a neighbor's house to borrow some bread. The neighbor shouted, "Do not bother me: the door is locked and my children are with me in bed; I cannot get up and give you anything." The man persisted, and got the bread (Luke 11:5–8).

We often find that our prayers bring about change, at least in ourselves, as God opens our eyes to a better future than we could have envisioned for ourselves. The Bible assures us that, with patience and courage, problems, failures, even tragedies can be turned into great blessings. In fact, James tells us, "Consider it pure joy, my brothers, whenever you face trials of many kinds. . . . Blessed are those who persevere under trial, because when they have stood the test, they will receive the crown of life that God has promised to those who love him" (James 1:2, 12).

As we pray continually, even during times when God seems distant and prayer feels fruitless, we immerse ourselves in the benevolence, grace, forgiveness, and love of God. Our attitudes toward life are modified accordingly. This doesn't mean that we become passive or weak. Living in harmony with the omnipotent God makes us stronger, just as seeing the world through the eyes of the omniscient God makes us wiser. And with this new strength comes an increased ability to apply in our lives the blessings given us by God, even in times of rejection, failure, or sorrow. Like Isaiah, we need to maintain our confidence in God's steadfastness, even in times of loneliness and apparent rejection, and constant prayer is one of the best ways to both express and nurture this confidence.

Communicating our questions, hopes, and fears in prayer makes them—even to ourselves—more open and clear; and the stronger the ties that bind us to God, the more likely we are to live, react, and behave in harmony with exalted standards—and with greater joy, peace, and happiness.

CHAPTER THIRTY-FOUR

Letting In the Lord

> When he was at the table with them, he took bread, gave thanks, broke it and began to give it to them. Then their eyes were opened and they recognized him, and he disappeared from their sight. They asked each other, "Were not our hearts burning within us while he talked with us on the road and opened the Scriptures to us?"
>
> LUKE 24:30–32

These verses are from the memorable stories about the appearances of Jesus to his disciples after the resurrection. They concern two followers of Jesus, Cleopas and his brother, who met a stranger on the road from Jerusalem to Emmaus on the day of Jesus' resurrection. The disciples spoke with the stranger about the sad events they'd witnessed, and they were amazed at his ability to explain everything in terms of the scriptural prophecies about the Messiah. They did not recognize that the stranger was Christ himself until the moment described in these verses.

In human terms, why do we suppose these followers didn't recognize Jesus? After all, this was a man they knew personally; they had lived with him, talked with him, and perhaps shared many a meal with their beloved teacher during the three years of his ministry. And in their overwhelming sorrow following his death, surely the image of his face and the sound of his voice were frequently in their minds.

We can imagine many explanations. They were traveling toward the end of the day, near sunset (that's why they invited the stranger to join them for supper); maybe the light wasn't good. They were sad and probably distracted by their grief; Luke says, "They stood still, their faces downcast" (24:17); maybe they didn't pay much attention to the stranger, who was just one of many pilgrims walking the same road. And it seems from other verses that Jesus looked somewhat different after experiencing death, burial, and resurrection.

Most significant, it seems that they were not ready to recognize Jesus. Luke says, "They were kept from recognizing him" (24:16). After all, this was a man whom they may recently have watched being buried. How could they be prepared emotionally to recognize the risen Christ and to experience the presence of God Almighty in the person of our Savior? Perhaps their blindness is understandable.

Is there any parallel between the experience of the followers on the road to Emmaus and our own lives? Yes, there are times when each of us fails to recognize the presence of Christ or the Holy Spirit. Remember that the Scriptures promise us that Christ is with us—at least potentially—not just as an occasional, miraculous event but at all times. In Revelation 3:20, he tells us, "Here I am! I stand at the door and knock. If anyone hears my voice and opens the door, I will come in and eat with him, and he with me." So an experience like that of the disciples, who recognized Jesus in the breaking of the bread, is always available to all of us.

Yet as we go through our daily lives, we often tend to keep the door closed to the presence of Christ. Perhaps we wait until a time of crisis, when we are sorrowful or afraid. Maybe we've had the experience of being ill and having a doctor tell us, "I'll call you when I have the test results," or "We'll soon know whether the cyst is benign or malignant." I've had such moments of anxiety, and I know it's human nature to remember God then; our prayers become especially intense!

We remember to acknowledge the presence of Christ in moments that are special. But how about when we are just traveling along the road, as the disciples were—driving home from work, on a shopping trip, or going on vacation? So often, we are like Cleopas and his brother. We don't open our hearts, our minds, and our imaginations to the powerful truth of our risen Lord.

Convinced as we are that the miracle of Christ's resurrection really happened some 2,000 years ago, we must consider this the most important event in the history of the universe. For us, it means that Christ still lives, that his spirit is still with us, and that we can build our lives around him as our Savior. If all this is true, then why do we so rarely acknowledge the presence of Christ? Perhaps it's because of our human tendency to select from our faith the things that are most convenient, most comfortable for us.

I want to be identified as a good, religious man, of course. If I'm an insurance salesman or a store owner, for example, and I live in a predominantly Christian community, I want to be known as a good church member. So I'll go to church, teach Sunday School sometimes, maybe serve as a deacon. Activities like this are relatively easy, and they make me feel good. But reaching out to the kinds of people Jesus chose—lepers, the mentally ill, prostitutes, thieves, blind people, the homeless—that's outside the purview of our normal Christian environment. It might put a burden on me, a burden of responsibility for someone else. And that's not nearly so convenient or comfortable.

So it's easy, even for dedicated Christians, to put off opening the door to Jesus. We want to be good Christians, but when it's more convenient, at least not today. "Just wait," we say, "until we reach retirement age—or our kids get out of college—or we make the last house payment. Then we'll try to put into our lives the kinds of things we would want to do if Christ were here."

But Christ *is* here, right now. And when we open our hearts to other people, particularly those who are different from us, we are opening the door to him. This is a practical way that Christians can take a major step toward realizing the constant presence of our Savior. He says so specifically: "As ye have done it unto one of the least of these, my brethren, ye have done it unto me" (Matthew 25:40).

When we take such a step, our eyes are opened, as were those of the disciples; we expand our lives, escape from the cages we build around ourselves, and enter a new environment of surprises, adventure, and real gratification. This is some of what Cleopas and his brother learned on the way to Emmaus. Imagine their elation and excitement! I wonder how long it took them to get back to Jerusalem, to share what they'd seen and heard with their friends? They might have set a 10,000-meter speed record!

We are thankful that the miracle they experienced isn't a mystery or a secret any longer. It's a truth all of us can share. Our Savior lives, and if we let it happen—if we accept his presence—our lives will be changed forever.

God's Riches at Christ's Expense

Chapter Thirty-Five

The Source of Courage

> The apostles left the Sanhedrin, rejoicing because they had been counted worthy of suffering disgrace for the Name. Day after day, in the temple courts and from house to house, they never stopped teaching and proclaiming the good news that Jesus is the Christ.
>
> Acts 5:41–42

Remember that these earliest Christians had no legal or civil authority: all political and military power rested with the ruling power of Rome, enforced by a governor and legions of Roman soldiers stationed in Israel. And closely associated with the Romans were the Jewish authorities, who had control over religious matters, led by the Sanhedrin, a kind of central committee of the faithful. And these civil and religious officials had ordered the disciples: "Do not preach anymore in the name of Jesus." Nonetheless, the preaching continued, even when the apostles were called before the Sanhedrin, threatened with death, and actually flogged for their disobedience.

Think of how the disciples reacted after the death of Jesus. It was a terribly painful and disillusioning event for them. Naturally, they were deeply hurt by the loss of their friend and teacher. But they were also very disappointed because of the apparent failure of Jesus' mission. Some of the apostles had believed they were following a man who was soon to become the ruler of the world. They could see themselves sitting by the side of the Messiah in an earthly kingdom, helping him rule nations: collecting taxes, running the government, giving orders to the army, even handing out welfare checks!

The death of Jesus shattered that fantasy. The powerful teacher whom they had revered proved to be fallible and vulnerable. The duality of his identity—both divine and human—suddenly shifted heavily toward the human side; he appeared not even as a strong and successful man but as a total failure, one who had been destroyed by the powers of the day. And with this apparent failure, the disciples saw their own future in jeopardy. Just having been associated with Jesus could put them in danger of losing their lives, or at least their freedom. Perhaps during this dark time after Jesus' death, Peter, who had been filled with remorse over denying Christ three times on the day of his death, thought, "I'm sure glad I didn't admit that I was one of his disciples."

Yet when we turn to this passage from the Acts of the Apostles, we find the disciples completely transformed. Oh, their names and appearances were the same, but they were new people, filled with hope and courage, eager to proclaim their faith in Jesus Christ in spite of the consequences. What caused this amazing change?

Two things had happened. One, of course, was the resurrection of Jesus. The effect of this event—the unprecedented conquest of death—on those who witnessed it cannot be overstated. And the disciples had shared multiple experiences of this miracle. It seemed clear, then, that his enemies had not conquered Jesus after all. Even death couldn't destroy him.

The second transforming experience the disciples shared was the coming of the Holy Spirit at Pentecost. This had been promised: "I will ask the Father, and he will give you another Counselor to be with you forever—the Spirit of truth" (John 14:16–17). In effect, Jesus had told his followers, "I can't be with everybody, everywhere, but the Holy Spirit can be with all of you at all times." And on the day of Pentecost, the Holy Spirit, symbolized by a violent wind, came upon all of the disciples, giving them renewed strength and a deeper, living sense of the presence of God. It was these two experiences—witnessing the resurrection and receiving the Holy Spirit—that gave the disciples the power to proclaim their belief in Jesus, even in a profoundly hostile environment.

It still takes courage to proclaim our complete faith in Christ. Most of us will never be called upon to make the kind of dramatic, life-or-death choice that the disciples had to make. So martyrdom is not a fate that many of us will face.

But always, Jesus set the example for us. When he reached out to people who were despised, different, lonely, or unattractive, and offered them his companionship, he was showing us the kinds of humble yet significant acts we can take in our daily lives that may require a great deal of personal courage. If we profess faith in Jesus, we should show it in our acts as well as our words.

The fact is that we have available what the disciples possessed: knowledge of the resurrection and the presence of the Holy Spirit. I'm still disturbed by a sermon preached in our church forty years ago. I don't remember anything except the title: "If you were arrested for being a Christian, would there be enough evidence to convict you?"

Chapter Thirty-six

Remembering to Be Thankful

Praise the Lord, O my soul;
all my inmost being, praise his holy name.
Praise the Lord, O my soul,
and forget not all his benefits.
He forgives all my sins
and heals all my diseases;
he redeems my life from the pit
and crowns me with love and compassion.
He satisfies my desires with good things,
so that my youth is renewed like the eagle's.

Psalm 103:1–5

Psalm 103 is a beautiful solo, a song of praise and thanks to God. The entire psalm is worth reading, but even the first five verses contain much food for spiritual thought, just a bit below the surface.

Giving blessings to God may not be as habitual for most of us as it should be. Maybe we say a prayer of thanks when we sit down for a meal. It's a good feeling when our small grandchildren argue about who can lead the family in saying, "God is great, God is good . . ." That's a fine way to begin. Memorizing and reciting a little phrase of thanksgiving is all right, but do we think about what it means? Are we thanking God for giving us the good things we enjoy, or are we asking God to bless our food? The two meanings are interrelated and quite compatible.

When the psalmist says, "Praise the Lord, O my soul," he intends that we should give thanks to God continually, not just on rare occasions. And the word *soul* carries more profound connotations than we may realize. For the ancient Israelites, "soul" meant the totality of a person's being, character, and life, including what we might call the heart and the mind. The psalmist is calling forth a blessing that arises from the depths of all that he is: "With all my heart and soul and mind," we might say, "Lord, I bless you."

The psalmist goes on to praise God for the benefits God has given him, and much of the rest of the psalm delineates those blessings. Consider, for example, verse 3: "He forgives all my sins and heals all my diseases." It's not easy for us to admit that we are sinners. When we do—when we ask God for forgiveness, as when we recite the Lord's Prayer—we may tend to do it superficially. We may say, "Lord, forgive our sins," and overlook the words "as [provided] we forgive those who trespass against us."

It's certainly easier to skip over our inadequacies than it is to acknowledge them specifically. We don't want to think about the times we are selfish or gossip about our neighbors. We don't care to recall the ways we're self-centered or callous toward people in need. But God remembers and (if we do) is ready to forgive all these sins and more. It is spiritually healthy to thank God for freeing us from them as the psalmist does.

It may seem strange, at first, that the same verse speaks about God's healing our diseases. But remember that in biblical times disease was often considered a form of punishment for sin. Job's suffering was blamed on sinfulness, as was leprosy in Jesus' time. So a leper was to be avoided, not just as a carrier of an infectious disease but as a person being punished by God for sins, presumably serious ones.

Most of us have, at one time or another, faced the possibility of death, either from disease or from other causes. At the age of three or four, I had colitis—often a fatal disease back then—and the doctor thought I was going to die. And when I was a submariner, there were three occasions when I could have died had my luck been just a little different. God has saved my life to this point. But I rarely stop to say, "God, thank you for the gift of life." Perhaps, like our sinfulness, our mortal frailty is something we don't often want to ponder.

Both of these gifts from God—the forgiveness of sins and the healing of diseases—relate to the renewal and refreshment of our lives. This idea is beautifully embodied in the image in verse 5: "He satisfies my desires with good things, so that my youth is renewed like the eagle's." Why like the eagle's? For us, the eagle is an especially powerful, handsome bird, which we use as a national symbol as well as an emblem of strength and beauty. However, the eagle had an additional meaning for the ancient Hebrews. Because it molts (sheds and regrows) all its feathers annually, they viewed the eagle as having a new life each year. For them, the eagle was something like the phoenix for us—a symbol of new life emerging from old.

How can we enjoy the gift of renewed life that the eagle symbolizes? No matter how old we may be, we can have a youthful exuberance about life, as did my mother even after she passed the age of eighty. Our sense of wonder at the beauties of nature need never diminish. Every day we can ask, "What can I learn about God's world that I don't yet know? What are some of the wonders of creation that I don't yet understand?" If we have inquisitive minds, we can continually grow in our appreciation of God's handiwork, no matter how many years we've lived.

The gift of renewed life can be enjoyed in the feeling of hope we have because of God's presence with us. We have surely known disappointment, sorrow, or failure, and the pain may have seemed unbearable. We may even have said, "I can't go on." Yet for most people, the passage of time heals those wounds, thanks to the sustaining love and grace of God. The ability to emerge with hope for a better day is another aspect of the renewed life God continually gives us. This, too, is a gift for which we should thank and bless the Lord.

Almost every day is filled with opportunities to be grateful. When we wake up in the morning, when we meet a friend, when someone lends us a hand, when one of our children or grandchildren expresses love, when we go to a job that is gratifying, when an unanticipated opportunity arises, when we see a beautiful sky, or when we have any kind of exciting experience—all of these are opportunities to give God the credit and acknowledge God's greatness. It's a good habit to develop.

CHAPTER THIRTY-SEVEN

Unseen and Eternal

> Therefore we do not lose heart. Though outwardly we are wasting away, yet inwardly we are being renewed day by day. For our light and momentary troubles are achieving for us an eternal glory that far outweighs them all. So we fix our eyes not on what is seen, but on what is unseen. For what is seen is temporary, but what is unseen is eternal.
>
> 2 CORINTHIANS 4:16–18

When we're children, the things around us seem permanent. Maybe it's because time passes more slowly for a child. I remember when a single afternoon of school seemed to last for days, and certainly the month before Christmas seemed to take forever.

I also remember good aspects of my life that I imagined would never—could never—change. One of these was the stability and strength of our family. The home that Mama and Daddy made for us children was the center of our lives, the place we returned to every evening, a haven whenever anything unpleasant or troubling happened. It was comforting to be able to return home to my parents when I got into a fight with another boy and had a bloody nose, or when I got a bad grade at school. (Well, I take that back. When I got a bad grade in school, I didn't want to go home to my parents!) Our family wasn't unique in those days. For most children growing up in Plains, the family was an unshakable foundation. When I left home to go to college, I had never heard of a divorced couple in our community. Divorce simply wasn't accepted; the assumption was that a binding oath had been made to God: a marriage was for life. We heard about people being divorced in Hollywood or New York, maybe, but never in Plains.

Today, of course, that has changed. Family instability and broken homes have come to Plains, just as they've come to small towns, cities, and the countryside everywhere in America. Is this change all bad? Not necessarily. Sometimes separation is the only option in a family where infidelity, abuse, or violence is an insoluble problem. But the lack of a solid home for children growing up today is a troubling thing.

When I was a boy, a trip to Americus, the nearest big town, was an adventure. The ten-mile round trip was generally an all-day affair, and we could count on getting at least one flat tire on the way. As for Atlanta, we'd go there every few years at most—a truly momentous event, perhaps to visit the enormous regional Sears, Roebuck store or to see the Atlanta Crackers play baseball. Travel was intimidating and difficult, but it also carried a degree of romance. The railroad engineer was an admired and envied figure. As a child, living two and a half miles out from town, I was excited to observe closely the six trains that went by our house each day, carrying freight and passengers to wonderful places all over the South. I'd often go out to stand near the track when the train was due and wave furiously at the engineer, and he'd wave back and maybe even toot his whistle for me. I'd have given anything to trade places with him!

Outwardly, our town hasn't changed much in the last century. We have about 700 people living in Plains, just as we have had for decades, and most of us make our living growing peanuts, pecans, pine trees, and cotton, or selling goods to the folks who do, just as we have for generations. But beneath the surface, life has changed in startling ways in southwest Georgia, just as it has all over America and the world. The descendants of people who in past generations might have lived in the same town for their whole lives now move from city to city every few years, pursuing work or school opportunities or simply seeking a better climate or a different lifestyle. Our children have lived in various parts of the country, and we frequently visit them, and also travel around the United States, Asia, Africa, Latin America, and other continents in my work on behalf of The Carter Center. It's a way of life that would have been unthinkable in my earlier days.

In my childhood, the radio was our only direct link to the larger world. When we got our first radio, we had no electricity in the house. We would hook up the big radio console to the battery from the car and gather around and look at the radio when our favorite programs came on. (I don't know why we looked at the radio, but somehow we felt we couldn't take our eyes from the dial and knobs.) Being able to listen to *Fibber McGee and Molly*, *Little Orphan Annie*, or *The Lone Ranger* as we sat in the living room of our farmhouse was a technological wonder for us. Now, even when we stay at home, our connections to other regions are vivid and instantaneous.

Greatly increased mobility and instant communications, throwaway marriages and broken families: these are just a few of the changes, good and bad, that we've seen in our lifetimes. In such a world, it's easy to lose the anchor of our lives, to become confused and uncertain about what really matters, or so obsessed with the rapidity of change that we lose sight of the changeless values that give our lives meaning.

I'm fond of quoting the wise words of Miss Julia Coleman, who was my high school teacher—words that I quoted in my inaugural address as president: "We must adjust to changing times, but still hold to unchanging principles."

In his second letter to the Corinthians, Paul addresses the same issue. He knew nothing about jet planes or the Internet, but he, too, lived in a world that seemed filled with complexities, troubles, and changes that were often unwelcome. His advice is not unlike Miss Julia's. He says we should fix our eyes not on what is seen but on what is unseen. For what is seen is temporary, but what is unseen is eternal.

What is seen is an ever-changing, confusing world, in which the only thing certain is that more changes will be coming tomorrow. But there remain unseen things that are truly permanent—more permanent even than the loving childhood home, built around my daddy and mama, that I never thought I would lose. The unseen, eternal things Paul had in mind are the values of which Jesus spoke: humility, compassion, justice, truth, friendship, and sacrificial love. When the world we live in today has passed away, the glory of these gifts will remain, unchanged and as precious as ever.

CHAPTER THIRTY-EIGHT

Facing Up to Sin

Blessed is he whose transgressions are forgiven,
whose sins are covered.
Blessed is the man whose sin the Lord does not count
against him
and in whose spirit is no deceit.
When I kept silent, my bones wasted away
through my groaning all day long.
For day and night your hand was heavy upon me;
my strength was sapped as in the heat of summer.
Then I acknowledged my sin to you
and did not cover up my iniquity.
I said, "I will confess my transgressions to the Lord"
and you forgave the guilt of my sin.

PSALM 32:1–5

Confession, I've found, is a topic that makes us uneasy. We may ask ourselves why we should want to get involved in something so unpleasant. After all, I've been profoundly blessed in my life. I have a nice family, a decent home, plenty to eat, a degree of comfort and security. If I'm so blessed, isn't it likely that there's a good reason for it? Maybe I've done enough to deserve it! And if I deserve all these blessings, what on earth could I possibly have to confess?

Well, we are blessed, it's true. We Americans, in particular, are a very fortunate people, with a high standard of living, a land abounding in natural beauty, and a degree of freedom rare in the world. But where do we get these wonderful gifts? Are they all our doing, or did our Creator have something to do with them?

Of course, we respond, our blessings come from God. And naturally we should be grateful. That's why we say a few words to thank God before meals—at least on holidays—and maybe give a few dollars to charity or to our church from time to time: to express our gratitude to God. But what does this have to do with confession?

The problem is that we can't be truly thankful unless we are willing to acknowledge our need for God. After all, if the good things we enjoy are our own doing—if we deserve them simply because of how hardworking, how decent, how special we are—then we really don't owe God anything. We can claim to be complete, needing no one and nothing outside of ourselves.

But we know, deep inside, that the reality is quite different. We realize that we're far from perfect, and we're willing to admit as much: Sure, sometimes I act and think in ways that don't make me proud. I focus too much on my own needs, and not enough on the needs of others. Sometimes, I admit, I'm not filled with compassion or love for those around me. If it's company policy, I'll bend the truth to make a big sale. And I even bear grudges against a few people. Yes, I'll admit all this. But confession? That's for sinners, isn't it?

The truth is, the standard set forth in the life and teachings of Jesus Christ is nothing less than perfection. Most of us have a great many blessings. Yet most of us would agree that our material possessions, and even our emotional and psychological blessings, like family and friends, are not enough to bring us complete peace and happiness. Think about it. Have we achieved the serenity and joy that comes from knowing we've fulfilled all the potential God has given us? Have we embodied in all our thoughts and actions the selfless love Jesus told his followers to share?

If the honest answer is no—as it probably is—then the gap between our lives and the model given us by Jesus is the source of that dissatisfaction, that uncertainty, that lack of fulfillment that makes us feel ever so slightly incomplete. And this resulting state is sin, which can only be fully healed through confession and forgiveness.

Fortunately, God's willingness to hear our confession and forgive us completely is inexhaustible. The Psalms, traditionally attributed to King David, express beautifully the human need for confession and the joy of forgiveness. Remember that David, one of the great heroes of the Bible, was very much a flawed, fallible human being. Whatever transgressions we may have committed in life, the chances are good that David did something even more wicked, from lying and adultery all the way to murder. How could this man, who violated almost every one of God's commandments, become a mighty leader of the Israelites? Through confession. Again and again, he repented and turned to God, freely admitting his wrongdoing and seeking forgiveness and new life. And each time, God granted him that gift. Without confession, our failings and transgressions become a heavy emotional and spiritual weight.

David describes this burden vividly: "My strength was sapped as in the heat of summer." We all know the feeling of uneasiness or even depression when we know we've done something wrong, yet cannot or will not acknowledge it. David understood this absence of joy and expressed it precisely.

But he understood, too, the relief that grows out of confession, and the new life that forgiveness makes possible: "Blessed is the man whose sin the Lord does not count against him and in whose spirit is no deceit." Notice the subtle shift between the first and second halves of this verse. The first part speaks of the joy of forgiveness: God no longer blames us for our sins, which are wiped away as completely as if they'd never happened. But the second half ("and in whose spirit is no deceit") places a continuing burden on the forgiven one. Perhaps we are reluctant to enumerate our sins. Maybe we're concerned that if we actually list them we'll remind God of some sins that have been overlooked in heaven! It's not enough to say, "Lord, I confess my sins," and then go right back to a life of selfishness, lying, gossip, and animosity, expecting to be forgiven again in the future. True forgiveness cannot exist without our most earnest effort to continue in that state of reconciliation with God, with a spirit devoid of deceit.

Will we fail again to live up to God's moral standard of perfection? We will, just as David did. Yet reconciliation and a new start are always possible, always available, if we are willing to acknowledge our transgressions and ask for God's help. The crucial first step—the most difficult one—is to admit our inadequacy and our need. It requires honesty and courage to do this. But if we can take that first step, God has promised total forgiveness.

CHAPTER THIRTY-NINE

Forgiving Ourselves

For I was alive without the law, but when the commandment came, sin revived, and I died. . . . For we know that the law is spiritual, but I am carnal, sold under sin. . . . In my flesh is no good thing, . . . for the good that I would I do not, but the evil which I would not, that I do. . . . O wretched man that I am! Who shall deliver me from the body of this death?

ROMANS 7:9, 14, 18–19, 24

There is therefore now no condemnation to them which are in Christ Jesus. For the law of the Spirit of life in Christ Jesus has made me free from the law of sin and death.

ROMANS 8:1–2

These are some of the most troublesome and beautiful verses in the Bible. Paul has been struggling in this letter to the Romans with the most basic concerns of a person's relationship with God. In my own Christian witnessing, I have used the verses "For all have sinned and come short of the glory of God" (Romans 3:23) and "For the wages of sin is death" (Romans 6:23). Romans 7 continues with the anguished cry of Paul, who struggles with a fruitless effort to resist the temptations that confront him as a fallible human.

Under a strict interpretation of the law, there is only condemnation, and no forgiveness. It is agonizing for devout people to contemplate the consequences of sin as we face a righteous God who cannot abide anything other than perfection. Before Christ, many devout believers made earnest but frustrated efforts to comply fully with literally hundreds of religious rules and regulations, in a futile effort to fulfill God's requirements.

Then, in Romans 8, came the glorious declaration: There is no condemnation to those of us in Christ Jesus! Let's think for a moment about the meaning of the word *in.* It has the connotation of being within a single body, a more intimate relationship even than that between a husband and wife. If I have a serious ear infection, for instance, I might be cured with an antibiotic injection. But it wouldn't help if the injection were given to my wife. Yet as Christians we are in Christ, and he in us. There is an extraordinary commonality that results from accepting Christ as Savior—living in Christ, with the Holy Spirit within us.

Baptism is a symbolic expression of being buried in Christ and raised to salvation. If we acknowledge our lack of self-reliance and reach out to God through faith in Christ, then God forgives us, completely cleanses us, and accepts us through grace. But grace is not a license to sin. We realize that, on the cross, Jesus assumed the punishment for our sinfulness or failures. With this realization comes an obligation, which we are often inclined to forget or minimize.

Suppose, for instance, I knew that the responsibility and punishment for all my selfishness, gossiping, animosity, jealousy, lack of compassion, or other sins would be borne by my daughter, Amy. Imagine the feelings of any parents, knowing that their sins would mean suffering and torment for their children. There is no doubt that they would be striving constantly to live better lives. Do we love Christ less than we love our Amys?

We have within us the strength to reject temptation. We are not dormant supplicants, but, as Paul tells us in Romans 8:37, "we are more than conquerors through him that loved us." The last two verses of this chapter are a powerful guarantee: "For I am persuaded that neither death, nor life, nor angels, nor principalities, nor powers, nor things present, nor things to come, nor height, nor depth, nor any other creature shall be able to separate us from the love of God, which is in Christ Jesus our Lord."

There could not be any more total assurance of God's total forgiveness. Then why can't we, like Paul, find a way to forgive others—and ourselves?

When the Road Is Rough

CHAPTER FORTY

Rejected Yet Loving

> O Jerusalem, Jerusalem, you who kill the prophets and stone those sent to us, how often I have longed to gather your children together, as a hen gathers her chicks under her wings, but you were not willing.
>
> LUKE 13:34

The note of longing in the voice of Jesus here makes his feelings toward the people of Jerusalem very clear. Having been rejected and persecuted by them, especially by their religious leaders, he was deeply saddened, yet the overwhelming sense of the passage is the deep, abiding love of Jesus for his people, even for those who had turned against him. It's an amazing combination of emotions, especially when we think back to the experiences of rejection in our own lives.

Virtually every person must live through crises of this kind. As a candidate for governor and president, I deliberately exposed myself to public rejection, but politicians who must face the voters are not the only ones. Think back, for example, to our earlier years. As little children, we are usually encapsulated in the aura of protection created by our parents' benevolent care. As teenagers, we begin to break away from parental control or influence, and there is a torn element in our lives. Part of us clings to the protection of our parents' love, while another part reaches out for new sources of approval. This can be a traumatic time for both generations. Teenagers may reject their parents completely, making them feel guilty and inadequate, even as the parents question their children's newfound values and strange tastes in music or clothes or friends. Perhaps a sustaining love can help to heal the breach in time, but these years when a young person struggles toward independence are often painful for all concerned.

And teenagers' groping for a new life will usually bring with it new experiences of rejection and hurt. Remember when we first fell in love? When I was twelve years old, I had my first sweetheart. Her name was Eloise, though we all called her Teeny. I'd take her out in my daddy's pickup truck—this was in the days before drivers' licenses were required—and we would have a good time together. That is, until a new boy, who had his own automobile, came to our school in Plains. His name was Lonnie. To my dismay, Teeny abandoned me and began going with Lonnie. Smarting from the hurt to my pride, and not willing to relate it to my own failure as a suitor, I always said it was because of the automobile.

When I was twenty-one and in my last year at Annapolis, I fell in love with Rosalynn on our first date. Six months later, I asked her to marry me, totally expecting her to accept. But she said, "No!" I was in abject despair until months later, when she mercifully changed her mind.

All of us, then, go through times of rejection. How do we cope with them? It's very difficult for us to absorb the realization that we have been rejected, either as individuals or for the ideas or beliefs we have, and still feel love and acceptance toward those who have turned away from us. The pain and embarrassment of being cast aside are usually just too great to bear, especially at first.

So it is remarkable to see, in both the Old and New Testaments, how steadfast is the love of God toward us, despite our unfaithfulness. The Hebrew Scriptures repeatedly tell of the Israelites' rejection of the mandates of God. Not only did the Jewish people ignore or reject the teachings of the prophets, but they even turned at times to the worship of other gods or idols of their own making. Through it all, God's love for the Israelites and faithfulness to the covenants remained strong. Jesus was referring to this history in these verses from Luke's Gospel. Like the prophets before him, Jesus had been rejected by the people of Jerusalem, incited, in his case, by the powerful high priest and other members of the Sanhedrin, who were concerned about maintaining their own power and authority in the nation.

Despite this, and in full knowledge of the painful destiny he would soon face, Christ spoke these words of longing when he was going toward Jerusalem and facing trial, rejection, and death. He was motivated by his love for the people there and by the hope that, in the fullness of time, they would be saved and retained in the fellowship of believers.

What does this mean for us today? The lesson is twofold, I think. First, when we feel rejected, perhaps unfairly, we should strive to follow the example of Jesus in being persistent in generous love, even for those who may be rejecting and unloving toward us. This is never easy, but our Savior lived through the worst of it, and his spirit will strengthen us if we ask for that help in prayer.

And second, we should always remember that, when we are the rejecting ones who turn away faithlessly from our Creator, God's love, faithfulness, and desire to forgive our sins and shortcomings remain unchanged. The whole history of God's relationship with humankind shows that we will never be abandoned. Our faith in Jesus Christ as Savior is the guarantee of this promise.

CHAPTER FORTY-ONE

Facing the Future

The Lord said to Joshua . . . "Be strong and courageous, because you will lead these people to inherit the land I swore to their forefathers to give them. Be strong and very courageous. Be careful to obey all the law my servant Moses gave you; do not turn from it to the right or to the left, that you may be successful wherever you go."

JOSHUA 1:1, 6–7

Remember Bert Lahr, the wonderful old comic actor who played the Cowardly Lion in *The Wizard of Oz*? He sang a funny song in that movie about the one quality he lacked—the one, he said, that could turn a slave into a king. That quality, of course, is courage. And courage of many kinds is a recurring theme in the Bible.

When we think of courage, we think first of physical bravery, thanks to movies about heroic crime fighters, soldiers, cowboys, and so on. King David, who fought Goliath, the powerful hero of the Philistines, exemplifies such courage.

Joseph is an example of moral courage. As a trusted slave in the house of Potiphar, an official of the pharaoh, he had the audacity to reject the sexual advances of Potiphar's wife. She was a beautiful woman who promised Joseph physical pleasure; political, social, and economic security; and personal advancement, if only he would betray his master. Yet he remained true to his principles and suffered imprisonment as a result.

Social courage is willingness to defy the standards or customs of our society in the name of a higher morality. Jesus is the supreme example of social courage. He gave his teaching, acceptance, and love to those generally considered least worthy of it: Gentiles, sinners, the sick, the outcast, and the despised. And he paid the ultimate price for his courage.

Joshua, who perhaps receives less appreciation than he deserves, gives us another example of courage. While Moses was relaying God's commandments to the Israelites, Joshua was fighting the battles. And unlike almost all the other Israelites, Joshua never deviated from his loyalty to God. So when Moses died, God chose Joshua to lead the Israelites into their promised land.

Think of how Joshua must have felt; imagine his trepidation, knowing that the fate of the Jewish people was now in his hands. The promised land, toward which they had journeyed for more than forty years, was still unknown, filled with unanticipated perils and enemy peoples. And the danger of rebellion or disobedience among the Israelites themselves was still strong. How could Joshua know whether he would be able to lead them in unity and faithfulness, when Moses himself had sometimes failed?

No wonder God, in these opening verses of the Book of Joshua, repeatedly admonishes him to have courage! But notice what else God says here. "Be careful to obey all the law my servant Moses gave you." The two instructions go hand in hand.

As we face changes and challenges, we need to hold on to the things that don't change, the foundations on which we can build our lives despite the uncertainty and danger of the future. God's law is the greatest of these foundations. Fear is a natural reaction to uncertainty; I myself don't like to face a challenge whose outcome can't be known. It sometimes seems that today's world forces us to cope with greater uncertainty than ever before. A sociologist recently found that average Americans now change jobs eight times in their lives. I've changed jobs at least that many times myself—from farmer to naval officer, nuclear engineer, farmer, businessman, governor, president, professor, author, and so forth. Each change of this kind requires courage; it forces us to take on new responsibilities, make new friends, and try things that may not succeed.

Long before we had tractors or even electrical power on our farm, I remember my father, a good and brave man, going outside at night and walking up and down in our yard, unable to sleep because he'd heard thunder in the distance. He knew that if it rained one more time, we'd probably lose the year's peanut and cotton crops. The destructive Bermuda grass, nut grass, and johnsongrass would take over, and the crop would be lost because we couldn't keep up with just mule-drawn plows. A religious man, my daddy prayed for some dry weather but also for strength and courage to deal with whatever came. Although the weather did not always suit him, the most important part of his prayers was answered.

The future is sometimes fearsome, and I haven't even spoken of the inevitable, devastating changes when friends and family are parted by death. Only the certainty of God's love can ultimately overcome the uncertainties of this earthly life.

When we are fearful about the future, Christ's message to us is the same one that God gave to Joshua: "I am with you, and the promises I have made shall certainly be fulfilled. But as you cross the river, be sure to follow my commandments, without swerving to the right or the left." If we do this, we can face the future with courage, no matter what unknown changes it may bring.

CHAPTER FORTY-TWO

We Underestimate Ourselves, and Others

Therefore, my beloved brethren whom I long to see, my joy and crown, stand fast in the Lord. . . . Rejoice in the Lord always; again I say, "Rejoice.". . . Be anxious for nothing, but in every thing by prayer and supplication with thanksgiving let your requests be made known to God. And the peace of God, which passes all understanding, shall keep your hearts and minds through Christ Jesus. . . .

I know how to get along with humble means, and I also know how to live in prosperity; in any and every circumstance I have learned the secret of being filled and going hungry, both of having abundance and suffering need. I can do all things through him who strengthens me.

PHILIPPIANS 4:1, 4, 6–7, 12–13

Paul was in prison, probably in Rome, when he wrote this letter to the small church at Philippi. He was hopeful of visiting the congregation again, but he was not to see them before his execution.

Paul expresses his hope in this letter that the church could overcome its difficulties and be united. He also says that he is concerned about other preachers who have made derogatory remarks about him but is still grateful that they are spreading the gospel.

The early Christians lived in turmoil, in a time of rapid change in the religious and philosophical world. It was only natural that there were serious divisions in the churches, as they struggled to survive and were bombarded by sometimes conflicting messages from Paul, Peter, Apollos, and other emissaries sent more directly from the church in Jerusalem. There was also intense competition and jealousy within the local congregations, particularly as Christianity became more acceptable and even popular.

Ours is a time of extremely rapid communication, and we are bombarded by conflicting voices on television and radio. In the Christian community—or communities—there are divisions, competition, and jealousy, and we face the kinds of personal challenges and fears about which Paul gives reassurance. Doubt about the future and particularly uncertainty about financial status is of concern to us all. We worry about whether we make $14,000 a year or $140,000 a year, when many people have to exist on $140 a year, or even less. Still, most of us are profoundly blessed with material things. We are not starving, our babies are not dying within a few weeks after birth, we don't sleep on the streets in human and animal filth, as millions of people in the world do.

In April 1997, Rosalynn and I visited a happy and relatively prosperous family who live near the top of a mountain about ten miles from Addis Ababa, Ethiopia. From the main road, we walked up and down a steep and twisting trail, and were welcomed in their home. It was just one room, about the size of a small bedroom in a working-class American house. The proud mother and her three children shared the space with their sheep and chickens, and they were laughing about a recent problem. The houses in the village had been wired with electricity, each having one light hanging from a cord. A well-meaning American friend had given this family a 100-watt bulb to replace the single dim bulb they had been issued. This had caused an overload, and the village lost power for two days. As punishment, the family was deprived of electricity for a month.

Their only income came from gathering fallen limbs from nearby eucalyptus trees and binding them into large bundles, which the mother would carry down the mountain to the city to sell for fuel. With the help of her children, she could make five round trips each week in good weather, producing a gross income of about three dollars. We walked over to her bundle prepared for the next day, which was about two feet in diameter and six feet long. Rosalynn could barely lift it off the ground, and I could never have put it on my back without help. We hated to imagine carrying it more than ten miles down the winding road to Addis Ababa. Yet this was a happy family, grateful to God for their blessings.

This was a vivid reminder to us of our tendency to be overly concerned about material things. We might also think of a few verses from the Sermon on the Mount: "Therefore take no thought, saying, 'What shall we eat?' Or, 'What shall we drink?' Or, 'Wherewithal shall we be clothed?'. . . for your heavenly Father knows that you have need of all these things. But seek first the kingdom of God, and his righteousness; and all these things shall be added unto you" (Matthew 6:31–33).

The point of these admonitions is summarized in the two words "seek first." All of us will have to face doubts, concerns, challenges, disappointments, sorrows, and apparent failures, as did the biblical heroes. Consider Peter, who denied Christ; Paul, who persecuted Christians; David, who committed murder to conceal his adultery; and Joseph, who was sold into slavery by his own brothers. For all of these, as there should be for us, there was an overriding priority of faith, a willingness to depend upon God for guidance through prayer, to sustain us in times of trial, and to forgive us when we repent.

Paul reminds us that this gives us not just an adequate existence but one of joy and all-encompassing peace. Regardless of our transient troubles, he says, "Rejoice in the Lord always; again I say, 'Rejoice!' "

Let's take a look at the man giving this advice. Paul was in prison, not knowing which day he would be executed because of his faith. He had been in jail several times and seldom received tangible support from members of the congregations he had helped to establish—he rarely even heard from them. Most churches were quite small, tiny enclaves of Christianity in large and mostly antagonistic communities. Paul was constrained to write a few letters that may or may not have been delivered, usually to a single member of one of the churches.

He had never preached to large and adoring crowds or been blessed with demonstrable success. Instead, as he told the Corinthians, five times he had been given thirty-nine lashes by the Jews, three times he had been beaten by the Romans, he had been stoned, shipwrecked on three occasions, often cold and hungry, and imprisoned several times. He could very well have looked upon his life as a failure.

Still, he gave the Philippians and us valuable advice about how to face our challenges. Don't be timid; instead, reach for greatness. If we're doubtful, get a partner, Jesus Christ. And remember, "I can do all things through Christ, who strengthens me." (Philippians 4:13)

CHAPTER FORTY-THREE

Our Favorite Disciple

Peter said unto him, "Lord, . . . I will lay down my life for your sake." Jesus answered him, "Will you lay down your life for my sake? Truly, I say to you, the cock shall not crow till you have denied me three times."

JOHN 13:37–38

When I first taught a Sunday School lesson based on this text, at First Baptist Church in Washington while I was president, I began by asking the class, "Who is your favorite disciple?" Almost unanimously, the response was "Peter!" And then they called out multiple reasons for their preference: "I feel at ease with him." "He's human." "He was rough-hewn, a fisherman." "Peter was impetuous, he overdid things."

"When he failed, he really failed." "He admitted it when he had doubts."

Strangely enough, the Bible tells us much more about Peter than about any other apostle, including the names of his father and his brother, that he was married, his profession, where he lived, and that John the Baptist strongly influenced him.

Peter had an intricate relationship with Jesus and a roller-coaster career, with soaring successes and abysmal failures. Our class had a long discussion about failure—something we all have to face. One comment was "Peter bragged too much, and failed often, because he tried a lot." Maybe it's natural for us to identify with him.

Thomas Edison, one of the world's greatest inventors, had a visitor one day and took him down to his basement laboratory to show him a new, experimental light bulb. Edison threw the switch and the bulb failed to light. The friend said, "Well, I'm sorry about your failure." Edison replied, "No, that was a success. Now I know one more thing that won't work."

One of our most admired politicians first ran for the state legislature in '32 with twelve other candidates. He came in eighth. Later he was elected, ran for Speaker, and was defeated badly. He left the legislature and tried to get an appointment as federal land commissioner, but someone else got the job. In '58, he ran for the U.S. Senate—and lost again. His life story was almost an unrelieved litany of failure. But two years later, Abraham Lincoln was elected president of the United States and became one of our nation's greatest political leaders.

So we relate to our leaders when they exhibit human weaknesses and failures. Despite Peter's shortcomings, other disciples seemed to recognize him as their leader, and Jesus seems to have been intrigued by him. Even today, we can see in this great apostle many of our own failings. Let's recall some of the events in his life and try to relate them to our own experiences.

Perhaps before other disciples, Peter knew who Jesus was and said, "You are the Christ, the Son of the Living God" (Matthew 16:16). But a few verses later, when Peter rebukes Jesus for predicting his own tragic fate, Jesus denounces him as "Satan." In our lesson text, John reports another swift change in the status of Peter, as he brags about himself only to be faced with the prediction of his betrayal of Christ. Shortly thereafter, Jesus went off to the Mount of Olives to pray. Knowing he was vulnerable to capture, he repeatedly asked his disciples to stay alert. More than once, Peter and the others went to sleep.

Peter was not afraid to express himself boldly, sometimes contradicting the statements of Jesus. He also had little reluctance to make public admissions of his doubts when they existed. One of the most poignant of these confrontations occurred at the Last Supper, when Jesus girded himself with a towel and began to wash the feet of his disciples. When it was Peter's turn, he said, "Lord, you will never wash my feet!" Jesus said, "If not, you will have no part with me." Taken aback, Peter responded, "Wash my feet, and also my hands and head" (John 13:3–9).

With all his good intentions, how could Peter make so many mistakes? His problem was similar to our own: He was filled with pride and considered himself self-sufficient—not needing God to help him withstand the inevitable human temptations. But he had faith, kept on trying, and eventually reached greatness in God's eyes.

CHAPTER FORTY-FOUR

The Span of Life

> Now there were some present at that time who told Jesus about the Galileans whose blood Pilate had mixed with their sacrifices. Jesus answered, "Do you think that these Galileans were worse sinners than all the other Galileans because they suffered this way? I tell you, no! But unless you repent, you too will all perish. Or those eighteen who died when the tower in Siloam fell on them—do you think they were more guilty than all the others living in Jerusalem? I tell you, no! But unless you repent, you too will all perish."
>
> LUKE 13:1–5

Why do bad things, even early deaths, happen to good people? And why do those who seem unrighteous sometimes enjoy long, financially prosperous lives? A few years ago in Alabama, a group was assembled in church preparing for their annual Easter pageant when a tornado struck. The building collapsed on them and twenty people were killed. Four were small children, excitedly anticipating the happy event; one was the four-year-old child of the church pastor. The timing and circumstances of this tragedy shocked Christians everywhere. How could innocent children be slaughtered in church, just a few days before celebrating the resurrection of Jesus Christ?

In one way or another, many of us have had to face the terrible question of premature, apparently unjust suffering or death of someone we know and love. When I first began teaching Sunday School at the Maranatha Baptist Church in Plains, there was a woman in my class whom I liked very much. She was a good athlete, and she and I would often go jogging early in the morning. Sometimes during class, I would glance at her and see tears running down her cheeks. I knew she had had a five-year-old son who had died, and something in the Bible lesson had reminded her of him. She had never overcome the torment of that personal tragedy.

Many people in biblical times had a pat way of dealing with this issue of incomprehensible suffering. They would claim that those who suffered (or perhaps their parents) were sinful in the eyes of God, even if no one could see what their sins were. The presumption was that God was punishing them for these sins. Disease was often attributed to evil spirits, or to moral and spiritual uncleanness. From this belief, it was a short, easy step to blaming victims for their suffering and ostracizing them so they wouldn't contaminate others.

Truth and falsehood are strangely intermixed in this doctrine of disease. It's true that some illnesses can be spread by human contact, which is why we have to take precautions when we encounter victims of contagious diseases. It's also true that many medical conditions are caused by human behavior. Unsafe sex, smoking, excessive drinking, poor nutrition, and the terrible living conditions of the poor and homeless all produce illness and suffering. People who fail to do what they can to free themselves from addictions and other self-destructive behavior help produce their own illnesses and death, and in that sense can be said to bring misfortune on themselves. But does this mean that they should forfeit our compassion and sympathy? I don't think so.

It's easy for us to become self-righteous in contemplating the suffering of others, especially when they have contributed to it in some way. It's comforting, too; it implies that, if we are well, we must be better, purer, stronger, or more moral than those others who are suffering. But common sense and reflection should show us that this belief, however tempting, is wrong. First of all, when measured against the only person who was without sin—Jesus Christ—all of us fall short of perfection. If illness or early death is a punishment for sin, then none of us should escape unscathed.

Second, it's plain that physical well-being and moral goodness don't go hand in hand. We all know people who have lived long, healthy lives without being moral paragons, while others have died young without doing anything to deserve such a fate. Jesus, of course, is the supreme example. His was the perfect life, a model of sinless love, but it was cut short at the age of about thirty-three by a death of unsurpassed cruelty and suffering. If Jesus' life is any indication, how can anyone claim that death and misery are generally imposed on those who deserve them?

We don't know the history behind Jesus' comments about the eighteen unfortunate people who were killed when the tower in Siloam fell on them. It sounds like a tragedy not unlike the tornado hitting the church in Alabama, or like many other calamities in the news almost every day. Jesus uses it as an example to warn his followers not to believe that those who suffer premature death have done something to deserve it. Were they, he asks, "more guilty than all the others living in Jerusalem? I tell you, no!" Yet Jesus goes on to say, "But unless you repent, you too will all perish." What can he mean?

Obviously, Jesus is not warning his followers that a tower will fall on them if they go on sinning. He has specifically disclaimed any such clear cause-and-effect relationship between suffering and sin. His message is subtly different from that. Don't concentrate, he says, on the number of years we have left on earth. At best, life is short, and its duration is unpredictable. Instead, concentrate on how we live—looking into our heart and soul and focusing on the most important questions: Who am I? Why was I created? And what am I doing to make my life on earth as meaningful as possible?

This is a difficult, challenging lesson. Death comes to all of us, and the time and manner of our death may not match what we think we deserve. We exaggerate the importance of longevity, with some people almost overwhelmed by fear of dying. But in the end, Jesus reminds us, the pain of earthly death is not the most important thing. What matters most is the eternal life that God has promised us. This is a gift that we can enjoy not just at the end of our earthly existence but beginning now, in the way we live each day. If we repent, have faith in Christ, and strive to embody his love and mercy in our own lives, we can overcome the fear of a future death in the joy and excitement of a present life that is ever more fully united with God.

God's Call

CHAPTER FORTY-FIVE

Running the Race

Therefore, since such a great cloud of witnesses surrounds us, let us throw off everything that hinders and the sin that so easily entangles, and let us run with perseverance the race marked out for us. Let us fix our eyes on Jesus, the author and perfecter of our faith, who for the joy set before him endured the cross, scorning its shame, and sat down at the right hand of the throne of God.

HEBREWS 12:1–2

We all grow up with particular dreams and ambitions. When I was a child, my friends and I wanted to be firefighters, policemen, cowboys, or train engineers. Nowadays, some kids want to become astronauts and fly through space, or to become star basketball players.

I grew up during the Great Depression years, a difficult time for us as it was for almost everyone. But my daddy was determined to send me to college, even though money was hard to come by and he himself had only finished the tenth grade. The only two options for me to receive a free college education were the service academies, Annapolis and West Point. So from the time I was five years old, when anyone asked me, "What do you want to be when you grow up?" I responded, like a parrot, "I want to go to Annapolis to the Naval Academy." And ultimately I realized that goal.

In Paul's letter to the Hebrews, he uses the famous metaphor of a race to describe the goals we choose to pursue in life. I don't know for sure what kind of race St. Paul had in mind, but for me, the proper image for our lives is not a brief event like a 100-meter dash. It's more like a cross-country race—a long, difficult trek over unpredictable terrain with hills, valleys, holes, roots, and other unexpected obstacles. It's a race that tests not only speed but also willpower and endurance.

Cross-country was my major sport at the Naval Academy. Years after I left Annapolis, when I became president, my cross-country coach was interviewed by a reporter from *The Washington Post*, and I must say that when I read the article, I couldn't recognize his description of my running—he greatly boosted my performance! I never called a press conference to correct his error, however. I just basked in the glory.

In cross-country racing, we ran and earned points as a team. The first runner to cross the finish line scored one point; the second finisher scored two points, and so on; the team with the lowest point total won the race. I had modest talent, so my personal expectation was not to finish first or second, but I struggled mightily to cross the finish line in a respectable time and help the team as much as possible. Perhaps there's a parallel here to the race of life we all run.

In many areas of life, each of us pursues different goals. Think back to the beginning of the first real job you ever had. Maybe you made a promise to yourself: "Someday, I want to be the chief executive officer of this company," or "Someday, I want to be the senior lawyer in this firm," or "Someday, I want to be the superintendent of all the schools in this county." It may be that you are still pursuing that goal, or a different career goal based on what you've learned about life and your own abilities.

It's important and worthwhile for us to have career aspirations. But goals like these have one thing in common: all define success by the world's standards. When we dream of success in our careers, we are thinking of yardsticks that are primarily material: income, prestige, or authority over others.

Because work is so demanding, most of us spend the majority of our time in pursuit of these worldly goals. There's nothing wrong with them, but because the world in which we live is so intensely competitive, with far more people pursuing top ranks than can possibly achieve them, we're almost inevitably doomed to some degree of failure. Not everyone can become the chief executive officer. Not everyone can sit in the corner office. With failure come frustration and, perhaps, feelings of inadequacy; and with intense competition come, at times, anger, resentment, jealousy, and alienation from those against whom we are struggling. So if the goals we pursue in life are purely of a secular nature, we are almost bound to be frustrated and, to a greater or lesser extent, unhappy.

Yet it's possible to pursue a successful career and also to develop goals and ambitions of a different kind—high objectives that we can certainly achieve and that lead not to a life of failure and unhappiness but to one of excitement, adventure, and achievement. These are goals we can observe in the teachings and life of Jesus Christ. Rather than driving ourselves daily with questions about why we have failed, we can shift our focus toward other concerns, to questions like: How can I draw closer to God? How can I reach out to people who are different from me? How can I more fully demonstrate justice, compassion, or friendship in the way I live this very day?

I think that, deep down, the most important goal most people share, whatever their career ambitions, talents, or lifestyle may be, is a simple one: to live in a truly meaningful way. We all know—and we feel with special poignancy as we grow older—that we have been given just one opportunity to live, a precious gift from God that we're eager not to waste. Are worldly ambitions or material possessions enough to satisfy our hunger for a meaningful life? Most of us who pause from the stresses of our daily existence to reflect seriously on this question must answer no. Fortunately, in the life of Jesus, we have another model: a way of living that does not pit us against other people but helps us unite with them in fellowship and love.

Not everyone can finish first in a cross-country race. And not everyone can play basketball in the NBA, win a Nobel

Prize, or make millions in the stock market. But everyone can be successful according to the standards of God. Each of us can honor God through our lives' commitments, in our activities, and through giving and sharing our time and talents with others. And the joy and excitement of a life built around these values is greater than anything money can buy.

C H A P T E R   F O R T Y - S I X

Responding to God's Call

The word of the Lord came to me, saying, "Before I formed you in the womb I knew you, before you were born I set you apart; I appointed you as a prophet to the nations."

"Ah, Sovereign Lord," I said, "I do not know how to speak; I am only a child." But the Lord said to me, "Do not say, I am only a child. You must go to everyone I send you to and say whatever I command you. Do not be afraid of them, for I am with you and will rescue you," declares the Lord.

JEREMIAH 1:4–8

There are times in life when we all need special strength. Some of those times are obvious: when a loved one dies, when we lose a job, when an especially great temptation assails us.

Less obvious is the special strength we need to acknowledge when God has a calling for us, and to respond to that call.

How do we know when God is speaking to us? It's not always easy. One of my daddy's favorite stories to tell his Sunday School students was about a boy who worked from daybreak to dark on the family farm. This boy got it into his head that he was destined to receive a call from God. Sure enough, one morning, as he worked in the field, he looked up at the sky and seemed to see clouds forming the letters "GOP." "That's my call from God!" he said. "It's telling me that I need to Go Out and Preach." So he left the farm and began preaching. But no one wanted to listen to his sermons; he was just no good at it. Only then did he figure out what the message in the clouds had really meant: "Go On Plowing."

In the case of the prophet Jeremiah, God's message was unmistakable. God sent a special presence to Jeremiah and even touched his lips, saying, "Now, I have put my words in your mouth" (Jeremiah 1:9). So God made it very clear that there was a prophetic mission for Jeremiah. How did Jeremiah react to God's call? As we see in the verses quoted at the beginning of this lesson, it was a profoundly disturbing message for him to hear. Put yourself in his shoes. Jeremiah was a young, bashful kid, not a trained orator or a political leader, and he was being told to serve as a prophet to the nations. Notice that plural, "nations." That may have included Ethiopia and Greece, or Egypt and Babylon, as well as Israel and Judah: an enormous task. So this was a shocking statement.

No wonder Jeremiah responded as he did: "I am only a child." He felt inadequate for the job God was sending him to do.

This was a typical reaction of many people we read about

in the Bible who are called to some special task. When God called Moses to lead the Hebrews out of exile in Egypt, he repeatedly protested: "What if they do not believe me or listen to me and say, 'The Lord did not appear to you'? . . . O Lord, I have never been eloquent, neither in the past nor since you have spoken to your servant. I am slow of speech and tongue. . . . O Lord, please send someone else to do it" (Exodus 4:1, 10, 13).

Like Moses, Jeremiah felt inadequate to the task God was assigning him. What was God's response? It was much the same as to other leaders of Israel, or the reassurance later given to Mary, the mother of Jesus: "Do not be afraid, Mary, for you have found favor with God" (Luke 1:30). In effect, God said to all the chosen people, "Don't worry about a lack of talent, or about a challenging and unpredictable future. Just have faith, and I will give you the strength and ability you need."

How does this relate to us? Jesus has made the same promise to each of us. He knew that he would not be present in the flesh to comfort and sustain us forever, but he promised us the strength of the Holy Spirit: "The Counselor, the Holy Spirit, whom the Father will send in my name, will teach you all things and will remind you of everything I have said to you" (John 14:26). Like Jeremiah, Moses, and Mary, we will have adequate help from God in knowing what to do when God wants us to act.

We don't need any extraordinary gifts to be called by God to a special purpose in life. We don't need to be eloquent, handsome, powerful, or influential. We simply need to be willing to do something necessary for God's purposes. And we can't wait for a vision or a voice from heaven. Jesus has already set an example of humility, service, and compassion that is a permanent call to all his followers.

The talent it takes to carry out God's plan may be something very basic. Perhaps it's a compassionate feeling toward someone in our neighborhood who is lonely or unlovable—someone to whom we can reach out in acknowledgment or friendship. Perhaps it's the willingness to share someone else's burden or challenge, especially if it's that of a person hard to love. Or maybe we can take the initiative to forgive someone against whom we hold a grievance.

Living a life of purpose, then, doesn't require what the world considers special talent—just a readiness to respond when God calls, as Jeremiah did, or to follow the example of Jesus. If we examine our own hearts, minds, and consciences, perhaps we'll recognize some simple things God has in mind for us to do, ways of reaching out to express God's love for the world around us. These will always be compatible with our talents and opportunities. And if we answer God's call, even though we feel inadequate, we will have the help and strength we need.

CHAPTER FORTY-SEVEN

Riding Freely

Then Jesus said to them all: "If anyone would come after me, he must deny himself and take up his cross daily and follow me. For whoever wants to save his life will lose it, but whoever loses his life for me will save it."

LUKE 9:23–24

These words of Jesus are among the most famous in the Gospels. They are also among the most troubling. They certainly warn us that suffering in some form is part of the ministry of Christ. But in practical terms, what does this admonition imply? What does it mean for us to take up our cross in following Jesus?

First, there is one interpretation many people make that I

think is wrong. Some people apply this verse to any kind of trouble. According to this reading, taking up our cross could mean suffering from cancer or arthritis, having an unhappy marriage, being expelled from school, or going bankrupt in business. Those who follow this interpretation would say that Jesus is urging us here to accept such tribulations with strength and courage. There's wisdom in that idea. All of us suffer pain, disappointment, even tragedy, and to turn a time of suffering into an opportunity to grow spiritually by disciplining ourselves to accept it bravely is a good thing and a powerful consolation. But it's a mistake, I think, to feel at such times, "Well, I'm suffering; therefore, I'm fulfilling Jesus' admonition to take up my cross."

Jesus is talking here not about the troubles that all creatures must face but rather about suffering for *his* sake, or, as he puts it in verse 24, "losing one's life for me." We don't suffer cancer or have an unhappy marriage for Jesus' sake. Jesus has a different kind of suffering in mind. On the other hand, we don't need to take Jesus' words literally. True, in too many parts of the world there is still persecution of Christians on account of their beliefs, and to this day there are martyrs who actually give up their lives in defense of the word of God. We honor them and their courage, as we should. But those of us who are fortunate enough to live in lands where we are free to teach and practice our faith are still called upon to take up our cross each day. How so?

The best way, I think, is by emulating Jesus' life so fully that we set ourselves apart from the world, even while we live in the world, loving and serving it. The Gospels show us that Jesus addressed the same kinds of daily problems we face today—disease, poverty, prejudice, loneliness, hatred—with generosity and love in a way that would be considered strange and wonderful, in his time and in ours. And we know how the world responded to him—first with praise and admiration, but then with rejection, contempt, and violence.

Living as Christ commands is not easy; sometimes it's not even safe. But we can try. If we work every day for the Lord, speaking out against injustice and hatred, freely sharing what we have, and constantly seeking opportunities to help those who cannot help themselves, we will probably not run the risk of losing our lives, as Jesus did, but we may suffer in other ways. Maybe people will think we're a little odd; maybe some will look down on us. If we're in business, maybe we'll lose a few customers, because some people may find that being around us makes them uncomfortable; maybe we'll lose some income when we pass up business deals our consciences can't approve. Maybe we'll even find ourselves isolated from some of our closest friends and family, who don't share our beliefs and values. To accept, with God's help, any of these forms of deprivation is one way to take up our cross. In each case, others must benefit.

Clarence Jordan, a man who has had a great influence on my life, is one of many modern examples of this lesson. Back in the 1940s, Jordan founded Koinonia Partners on a farm not far from my hometown of Plains, Georgia. Koinonia was a biracial community, one of the few places in the Deep South where white and black people could live, work, and worship together at that time. It was not easy for them. The local merchants boycotted their farm produce, and members of the Ku Klux Klan attacked the farm more than once. They were falsely accused of being communists. But the residents persisted, demonstrating to the world that whites and blacks could live together in peace and friendship. This was the birthplace of the self-help movement known today as Habitat for Humanity.

Someone once asked Clarence Jordan whether he'd ever participated in the famous freedom rides during the civil rights movement of the 1960s. "No," he replied, "but I've always ridden freely." Jordan had an ethical, moral, and spiritual standard for his life, and he lived by it boldly. Sometimes it brought him acclaim, and at other times it brought him brickbats—or worse. But no matter what, he followed faithfully what he believed God was calling him to do. If we live out this philosophy of riding freely, declaring, "I'm going to follow the path God has laid out, no matter what the outcome," there are times we'll get into trouble and maybe even suffer deeply in mind or body as a result. But, of course, we can all expect to suffer in life anyway—isn't it better to suffer for good rather than for evil? (Peter makes this very point in one of his epistles—see 1 Peter 4:12–16.)

And Christ promises us that when we do take up his cross, we're following him on the only path that leads, in the end, to life.

CHAPTER FORTY-EIGHT

The Unfaithful

> She is not my wife, and I am not her husband—that she put away her whoring from her face, and her adultery from between her breasts, or I will strip her naked and expose her as in the day she was born. . . . Upon her children also I will have no pity, because they are children of whoredom. . . .
>
> Therefore, I will now allure her, and bring her into the wilderness, and speak tenderly to her. From there I will give her her vineyards, and make the Valley of Achor a door of hope. There she shall respond as in the days of her youth.
>
> HOSEA 2:2–4, 14–15

The contrast between these two statements is startling when we realize that in both it is the prophet Hosea speaking to his children and about the same woman, his wife, Gomer. God had instructed Hosea to marry her, in spite of the fact that she was known to be a whore—and she continued her prostitution after their marriage. As a cuckolded husband, Hosea had full legal authority to strip her naked and cast her out of the family's home.

The Book of Hosea contains an almost inseparable interweaving of his anguished cry to his children and the voice of God, who calls out to a remnant of faithful Israelites. This unhappy marriage relationship parallels that between God and the unfaithful people of Israel.

The text reveals that Gomer received nice rewards from her lovers, including food, clothing, and drink. And we learn that the Israelites also had a good life at this time (about 700 B.C.). They were prosperous, free, and at peace. However, they thought that their blessings came from the pagan god Baal, whom many of them were worshiping. In effect, they were saying to Jehovah, "We don't really need to retain our somewhat restrictive relationship with you, because we have much more freedom with other gods and still have good crops."

The troubling aspect of the lesson on unfaithfulness is that we're not supposed to equate ourselves with God or Hosea but with Gomer. In order for us to be faithful, there must be a commitment for us to honor—otherwise, there's nothing to betray. Marital vows are not the only kind; many types of commitments shape our lives. What is the origin of these restraints, goals, obligations, and promises? Beginning as infants, we absorb them from our parents, siblings, friends, teachers, from religious experiences and training for our professions, and from government laws, rules for athletic contests, and other accepted norms. If we have never read a Bible, listened to a sermon, or heard the name of Jesus, Moses, or Isaiah, we should still know God through our awareness of what has been created and of apparently unexplainable miracles. At each stage in our development, we are constrained by potential punishment and encouraged by rewards. We must choose whether to obey the rules or face the consequences for flouting them.

But we also have higher standards available to us that are purely voluntary—elements of idealism that transcend simple duties or obligations. These can come to us through various forms of affection, as we experience when we become infatuated with a sweetheart and feel this evolve into sacrificial love. An equivalent feeling can exist for our children or our grandchildren. These relationships are usually reciprocal, and the pleasure they create for us is a reward for our faithfulness.

We might be guided by a still more exalted standard, when we are willing or even eager to exceed normal expectations, perhaps with some sacrifice of our own well-being and without our admirable acts even being known. This is the highest form of moral aspiration.

Where do we derive these most transcendent ideals? For Christians, they come primarily from our knowledge of the life of Jesus Christ, who set a standard of perfection, generosity, gentleness, humility, service, compassion, and love. In what ways, then, are we unfaithful? As Christians, we are unfaithful when we betray or ignore the teachings of our Savior, all of which are designed both for our own good and for the benefit of others. Even the miracles of Jesus were not earthshaking or designed to exalt his own stature or to prove that he was the Messiah, but they set a moral example for us, emphasizing our commitment to alleviate suffering and to rescue the lonely and the despised.

Like Gomer, then, we are all unfaithful and deserving of separation from God. Yet just as Hosea reached out to his unfaithful wife, God reached out to the unfaithful Hebrews. In the same way, we know that Christ is reaching out to us, even though we do not persistently honor our commitments as Christians. Our forgiveness through Christ is total, as was Gomer's when Hosea said she would be "as in the days of her youth," when she was still a virgin.

In all cases, forgiveness has not been earned, but redemption has been made possible through grace, mercy, and love. This is a difficult story, but it's still beautiful.

CHAPTER FORTY-NINE

The Lord Looks at the Heart

> Samuel consecrated Jesse and his sons and invited them to the sacrifice. When they arrived, Samuel saw Elias and thought, "Surely the Lord's anointed stands here before the Lord." But the Lord said to Samuel, "Do not consider his appearance or his height, for I have rejected him. The Lord does not look at the things man sees. Man looks at the outward appearance, but the Lord looks at the heart."
>
> 1 SAMUEL 16:5–7

The story of Saul, Samuel, and David, and how the kingship of Israel came to be transferred from Saul to David, is a fascinating study of power, legitimacy, authority, and obedience—issues that cause us to ponder and speculate to this day. Of course, for the author of the biblical books of Samuel—and for believing Jews and Christians today—God's will is supreme and is the measuring rod against which the fallibilities of humans must be judged.

In the fifteenth chapter of 1 Samuel, just before the passage quoted here, King Saul, with the help of God, has won victory over the Amalekites. But the king is rejected because he disobeys God by sparing Agag, king of the Amalekites, and the best of their sheep and cattle. God tells the prophet Samuel, "I am grieved that I have made Saul king, because he has turned away from me and has not carried out his instructions" (verse 10).

It's somewhat troubling to us to see God demanding ruthlessness in battle. Looking ahead through the centuries, it's impossible to imagine Jesus, with his message of mercy and forgiveness, making a similar demand. But whatever we might think of God's order to Saul, the fact that he failed to obey it meant that Saul no longer merited the kingship.

God then sent Samuel to Bethlehem, saying, "I have chosen one of Jesse's sons to be king." Samuel was supposed to anoint, on God's behalf, the one whom God would reveal. We now know who the chosen one will be, but Samuel does not know. When he sees Elias and the other sons of Jesse, he assumes that it will be one of them. But God has in mind the youngest, David, who is off tending the sheep when Samuel arrives.

I think we can identify with each character in this story: Saul, because we have all been disobedient and failed to live up to a responsibility we have been given; Samuel, whose difficult task is to speak of God's wishes despite condemnation and danger; and the sons of Jesse, each a promising young man hoping to be exalted by God's favor. But in a different way, all of us are called to fill the role of David, who becomes God's anointed.

The Bible refers to every Christian as a saint. That doesn't mean we are perfect; we all know we're not. It means that we are set aside for the service of God; anointed, spiritually if not physically, as God's servants on earth.

What qualified the youthful David to be chosen by God? At the time, he was not a fine warrior, charismatic leader, or wise thinker, nor did he have a track record of notable achievements that would justify his selection as king. He did not exhibit the personal qualities that we think of as marking a leader. He didn't take the initiative or ask to be chosen but was just minding his own business, taking care of the sheep. But through Samuel, God sent for him. It was God's choice, not David's, that David should be anointed.

With God's presence, through the power of the Holy Spirit, each of us is given the potential of exaltation, of greatness—not greatness in the sense of fame or glory, with headlines in the newspaper or stories on the TV news about our deeds but, rather, the greatness that God measures. The Lord looks at the heart, we are told. There are simple things about us that might never be known by most people: what we think, what we pray, how we feel, the small, meaningful things we do—or fail to do—for another person. In God's eyes, these are the deeds for which we are anointed, and they may make us worthy of exaltation.

Saul fell from God's grace because of his arrogance in disobeying God's command. To replace him, God chose one of the humblest of his servants, the youngest son, the shepherd boy—who was destined for greatness. Centuries later, Paul wrote about God's choices in his first letter to the Corinthians: "God chose the foolish things of the world to shame the wise; God chose the weak things of the world to shame the strong. He chose the lowly things of this world and the despised things—and the things that are not—to nullify the things that are, so that no one may boast before Him. . . . Therefore, as it is written, 'Let him who boasts do so in the Lord' " (1 Corinthians 1:27–29, 31).

If we strive, whether persistently or only intermittently, to serve Christ, there are many things that need not worry us. We don't have to worry about how wise or clever we are—God chose the foolish. We don't have to worry about how powerful we are—God chose the weak. We don't have to worry about how popular we are, or even whether we'll amount to anything much—God chose the despised and the ones who are nothing. None of those human measurements counts when it comes to performing great acts in life—great acts as defined by God, acts of humility, obedience, and love.

CHAPTER FIFTY

Real Wealth

Jesus said to his disciples, "I tell you the truth, it is hard for a rich man to enter the kingdom of heaven. Again I tell you, it is easier for a camel to go through the eye of a needle than for a rich man to enter the kingdom of God."

MATTHEW 19:23–24

God creates us with a variety of needs, desires, interests, talents, and opportunities. But these things don't define what we'll be. They're like the bricks, lumber, wallboard, shingles, and tiles we might see piled on the road near a construction site. It's what we make from the raw elements of our personalities that defines who we are; and this is where priorities and choices are crucial.

In these well-known words of Jesus, our Lord is warning us about the importance of setting the right priorities in our lives. I don't think Jesus is opposed to money or material possessions as such; what concerns him is the tendency we have to equate our material possessions with what is valuable. The problem in both cases is making some material thing more important in our lives than God—an idol, in effect.

We don't have to be wealthy to fall into that trap; a person can be just as covetous by being focused on small things as by hoarding millions of dollars. What material things receive an inordinate amount of attention in our lives? For some of us, they may be the latest car, the finest kitchen equipment, or the property that adjoins ours. Some of us feel undressed unless we're decked out in the latest fashions; others feel our lives are empty unless we travel to some new, exotic place twice a year. One of my weaknesses is for computers. I enjoy working on a word processor (I write my poems and books on one in my office at home), I find E-mail a fast and easy way to communicate with our family, and I use the Internet to locate information that would otherwise require research in a library. I guess I'm on my fifth computer now. No sooner do I get acquainted with one than I want a newer machine that is faster, has more vivid images, and can do things my current one can't do.

None of these desires is bad in itself. But material wealth can be a particularly treacherous priority for us, especially in our society, where advertising and the media remind us constantly of the pleasures and prestige of consumption. The more we are interested in amassing things, the more we are thrown into competition with others—our neighbors, our colleagues at work, our adversaries in business. There will always be something I covet that I can't have, and when this happens I'm immediately tempted to engage in disputes, conflicts, and jealousy. And the more I focus on increasing my own store of possessions, the less I'm inclined to think about sharing my time, talent, or treasure with others. After all, being generous won't help my bottom line!

So the pursuit of wealth, while natural and harmless in itself, can carry serious spiritual dangers.

One way of testing whether our priorities are correct is to get into the habit of speaking to God, in prayer, about the things we want. If we take prayer seriously and really open ourselves to the presence of Christ whenever we pray, we'll find that our desires and wishes will be directed into channels that are truly nurturing and healthy. Imagine kneeling in your bedroom and praying, "In the name of Christ, my Savior, let me obtain a new computer or automobile, or the farm next door." Prayers like this sound wrong, almost shockingly so. We all have self-centered desires like these, but if we try to share them with God, their shallowness becomes apparent.

We need to accept Jesus as our partner in setting priorities. Prayer can help us do that. When making our needs and desires known to God, we are most often praying in the transmitting mode—speaking and not listening to God. Yet if we're sincere, we can't help but sense God's response and reaction to the desires we express; we shift, almost automatically, into the receiving mode. It's one of the benefits of habitual, daily prayer.

There's nothing bad about a shiny car, a nice house—or a powerful new computer! But before we focus all our time and energy on seeking these goals, we should try bringing them before God in prayer. As we shape and mold our desires, we may find ourselves pursuing the simple spiritual riches more avidly than costly material things.

CHAPTER FIFTY-ONE

If We Have Faith, Let's Show It!

What good is it, my brothers, if a man claims to have faith but has no deeds? Can such faith save him? Suppose a brother or sister is without clothes and daily food. If one of us says to him, "Go, I wish you well; keep warm and well fed," but does nothing about his physical needs, what good is it? In the same way, faith by itself, if it is not accompanied by action, is dead.

JAMES 2:14–17

The letter of James is one of my favorite books in the Bible. But through the ages, it has been a controversial part of Scripture. Martin Luther, the great churchman who helped start the Protestant Reformation, was so dubious about James's message that he called it "an epistle of straw." James continues to have his detractors, especially regarding the issue of faith versus works, about which he writes more than any other New Testament author. Some people say that James puts works—that is, deeds of charity, courage, and compassion for others—ahead of faith, or even substitutes works for faith. After I wrote *Living Faith*, there were letter writers who made the same accusation about me. I've thought about these letters, and believe that the criticisms are unjustified, certainly about James. As we'll see, he wanted us to understand that both works and faith are important in the life of a Christian, and that we can't have true faith without good works, and vice versa.

It's clear that an imbalance between faith and works is a constant danger. Some of us get so proud of our works that we think that's all there is, and neglect our spiritual lives—prayer, worship, fellowship, and study. We sometimes seem to place our works above Christ's supreme sacrifice as our path to salvation—as though we can earn a place in heaven by being so good that God is actually in our debt. This attitude is obviously wrong; it devalues the grace of Jesus, which is given to us without being earned and which we can never deserve, because we all fall so far short of moral and spiritual perfection.

Yet as James tries to show, the opposite attitude is equally wrong, when we place our faith so far above works as to imply that good deeds are unnecessary and unimportant. All we need to do, we believe, is walk down the aisle of the church during a revival meeting when we're ten or eleven years old and accept Christ as our Savior, and from then on just being regular church members meets our obligations as Christians. Some of us even go a step further and think all this is preordained—that we have been selected for eternal life while others never even have this opportunity.

On an institutional scale, we see this kind of attitude infecting some of our most famous and outwardly most successful churches. I think of a particular church in one of the big cities of the South. The new building cost $35 million, complete with all the pleasures of a huge health resort to serve the congregation, which is large and growing by leaps and bounds. Unfortunately, at the same time the new facility was being built, members canceled plans for an outreach ministry in an inner-city neighborhood, saying they couldn't afford it. I guess the expense would have interfered with the building of their sports complex.

Don't misunderstand; I don't see anything wrong with physical fitness or with ministering to the needs of our own congregations. But there is something wrong with becoming so committed to caring for our needs and pleasures that we forget about the practical ministry of Jesus Christ. It's also nice when membership rolls increase, but some churches grow because joining them is like gaining membership in a huge fraternal order or a country club.

That's the danger James is warning us against. James isn't saying that faith is unimportant. He's saying: If we have faith, let's show it! Prove it as Jesus did, by ministering not only to those like us, our friends and neighbors, but to the poor, the hungry, the lonely, and the despised. Become active, inquisitive, questioning, adventurous Christians. Take some of the blessings God has given us—our time and talents, our education, our financial status, our security—and say, "I want to invest this, in the name of Christ, in the same way that Jesus invested all that he had for us."

How do we do this? What's a practical way to reach out to someone in need or trouble? It depends on us—our background, our neighborhood, the amount of time and the specific talents we have to offer. Each of us has something unique and valuable to give. A habit of very small things is much more important than a few dramatic ones. We can make a gesture of forgiveness to someone against whom we've had a grudge; offer friendship to someone who is lonely or neglected; volunteer to be a big brother or sister to a local kid in need of guidance, or give time at the nearest hospital.

Or join one of my favorite organizations, Habitat for Humanity and work side by side with some of the poorest people in the world, helping to provide them with decent homes. There are Habitat projects in over 1,300 U.S. communities and more than 45 foreign countries. Habitat has branches on 450 college campuses and at over 100 high schools. Almost anywhere, we can help Habitat build a better world.

There are many ways to put our faith into action, limited only by our imagination. In the end, James's message is a simple one. To be saved, we need faith, surely; but self-satisfaction and self-glorification are not the end of faith. Rather, service to others, compassion, and justice exemplify the Christian life. When we emulate Christ by working to make these things real in our lives, we strengthen our faith as well.

CHAPTER FIFTY-TWO

Take a Chance

Whoever watches the wind will not plant;
whoever looks at the cloud will not reap. . . .

Sow your seed in the morning, and at evening let not your hands be idle, for you do not know which will succeed, whether this or that, or whether both will do equally well.

ECCLESIASTES 11:4, 6

As a person who grew up and still lives in a farming community, and has done his share of planting, cultivation, and harvesting, I find these images from Ecclesiastes particularly intriguing. And because of the provocative, even paradoxical nature of their message, more than one interpretation is possible. Let me share some of my thoughts about these curious, fascinating verses.

In a way, it would be easier to understand the author if he had written, in verse 4, "Whoever does *not* look at the clouds will not reap." That would just be a basic piece of farming wisdom. Any farmer in South Georgia knows that our crops will suffer if we don't pay attention to the weather. If we plant our peanuts when the ground is too cold or wet, the seed will rot; if we get a long dry spell, they won't sprout. So the smart farmer does pay attention to clouds, winds, rain, sun, and all the other weather signs. What, then, does the writer mean by seeming to say just the opposite?

I think he is warning us about the danger of seeking perfection in our lives. The farmer has to watch the weather signs, sure. But if we watch and ponder the weather and the other conditions too closely—if we measure and remeasure the humidity, the temperature, and the soil conditions—if we seek out and pay attention to all kinds of advice from every farmer, seed salesman, or extension service expert in the county—we may end up in a quandary, wondering, "Is this the right day to plant? Will tomorrow be better, or the day after that, or the day after that?" Before we know it, the time for sowing will be gone.

So if we wait for perfection in our lives, for exactly the right moment, then we may never act! This message applies to all of us.

If we've made a commitment to faith in Christ, we've promised to serve God according to the pattern Jesus set. Yet how many of us are really living that way? Instead, we wait for a better time. It's not deliberate; it just happens, year after year. And then there's retirement—we've got to be sure we have enough set aside for that, too, don't we? Before we know it, our lives have slipped away, with the commitment to serve God in Christ permanently on hold while the worldly things take precedence.

Ecclesiastes is warning us not to let that happen. Don't wait until everything is perfect before we act; in an imperfect, uncertain world, be bold! Go ahead!

Verse 6 gives another perspective on the same theme. It's often difficult to take risks in life. How do we know which seeds will grow best if we plant them? Will we succeed or fail at what we try? Maybe it's better not to take a chance rather than accept the possibility of failure.

Of course, that attitude leads to a timid, diminished life. Failure is a reality; we all fail at times, and it's painful when we do. But it's better to fail while striving for something wonderful, challenging, adventurous, and uncertain than to say, "I don't want to try, because I may not succeed completely."

In September 1994, when Sen. Sam Nunn, Gen. Colin Powell, and I returned from Haiti, having helped to resolve the crisis caused by a military coup and avoided the need for a planned U.S. invasion, President Clinton admitted that he'd never believed our mission could succeed. And frankly, there were times we'd felt the same way. During the thirty hours we spent in Haiti desperately trying to negotiate a settlement, there were at least four occasions when it seemed that the discussions had broken down and war was inevitable. But people in Port-au-Prince and Washington refused to give in to despair, and a settlement was reached that gave victory—and peace—to everyone concerned. It was not a miracle, just the result of human beings persisting in the face of uncertainty and risk, being willing to take a chance.

Every life offers similar opportunities. "Should I reach out to that man who hurt me deeply with an ugly comment or a cruel deed several years ago? Perhaps I could call him on the phone or knock on his front door, offering reconciliation and a chance at renewed friendship. But that would be a risky thing to do. What if he slams the door in my face, or shouts 'Go to hell!' and hangs up the phone? Maybe it would be better not to try!"

The Book of Ecclesiastes offers an antidote to that attitude. We'll never know whether something new and wonderful is possible unless we try. Let's stretch our hearts, stretch our minds, be adventurous! Serve God with boldness, and who knows what wonders the Lord may work?

Index of Scriptural References

Index

ABOUT THE AUTHOR

JIMMY CARTER, thirty-ninth president of the United States, was born in 1924 in the small farming town of Plains, Georgia, and grew up in the nearby community of Archery. His father, James Earl Carter, Sr., was a farmer and businessman; his mother, Lillian Gordy, a registered nurse.

After receiving a B.S. degree from the United States Naval Academy in 1946, he served as a submariner in both the Atlantic and Pacific fleets and rose to the rank of lieutenant, working under Admiral Hyman Rickover in the development of the nuclear submarine program.

When his father died in 1953, he resigned his naval commission and returned to Plains. He worked his own farm, and he and his wife Rosalynn operated Carter's Warehouse, a farm supply company. He was elected to the Georgia Senate in 1962 and was elected governor of Georgia in 1970.

In 1975, Carter was elected president of the United States, serving from 1977 to 1981. Noteworthy accomplishments of his administration included the Camp David Accords, the treaty of peace between Egypt and Israel, the SALT II treaty with the Soviet Union, and major domestic programs in education, energy, and environmental protection.

In 1982, he founded The Carter Center, a nonpartisan and nonprofit organization that addresses national and international issues of public policy. Carter Center fellows, associates, and staff join with President Carter in efforts to resolve conflict, promote democracy, protect human rights, and prevent disease and other afflictions throughout the world.

Mr. Carter is the author of twelve books, including the spiritual autobiography *Living Faith* (1996). Jimmy and Rosalynn Carter are the parents of three sons, Jack, Chip, and Jeff, and a daughter, Amy. They live in Plains, Georgia.